DESIGNED FOR HABITAT

Designed for Habitat: New Directions for Habitat for Humanity presents 12 new projects designed and built via collaborations between architects and Habitat for Humanity®.

The ways in which we think about affordable housing are being challenged by designers and not-for-profit housing advocates such as Habitat for Humanity and its affiliates. The projects chronicled in this book consider home affordability through the lens of monthly homeownership expenses, energy efficiency and residential energy use, and issues of designed resilience to natural events ranging from aging and accessibility concerns to natural disasters and climate change. New to this edition, the projects reflect new approaches to building scale, construction technology, energy and affordability, and design and context. Illustrated with over 100 color images, the case studies include detailed plans and photographs to show how these projects came about, the strategies used by each team to approach the design and construction process, and the obstacles they overcame to realize a successful outcome.

The lessons and insights presented will be a valuable resource, whether you're an architect, an architecture student, a Habitat affiliate leader, or an affordable housing advocate.

David Hinson is Professor and Associate Dean in the College of Architecture, Design and Construction, Auburn University, USA.

Justin Miller is Professor and Head of the School of Architecture, Planning, and Landscape Architecture, Auburn University, USA.

DESIGNED FOR HABITAT

New Directions for Habitat for Humanity

Second Edition

David Hinson and Justin Miller

NEW YORK AND LONDON

Designed cover image: Mueller Row Townhomes, Michael Hsu Office of Architecture.
Photographer: Chase Daniels

First published 2023
by Routledge
605 Third Avenue, New York, NY 10158

and by Routledge
4 Park Square, Milton Park, Abingdon, Oxon, OX14 4RN

Routledge is an imprint of the Taylor & Francis Group, an informa business

© 2023 David Hinson and Justin Miller

The right of David Hinson and Justin Miller to be identified as authors of this work has been asserted in accordance with sections 77 and 78 of the Copyright, Designs and Patents Act 1988.

All rights reserved. No part of this book may be reprinted or reproduced or utilised in any form or by any electronic, mechanical, or other means, now known or hereafter invented, including photocopying and recording, or in any information storage or retrieval system, without permission in writing from the publishers.

Trademark notice: Product or corporate names may be trademarks or registered trademarks, and are used only for identification and explanation without intent to infringe.

First edition published by Routledge 2012

Library of Congress Cataloging-in-Publication Data
Names: Hinson, David (David W.), author. | Miller, Justin (Justin Knowles), author.
Title: Designed for Habitat : collaborations with Habitat for Humanity / David Hinson and Justin Miller.
Description: Second edition. | Abingdon, Oxon : Routledge, 2023. | Includes bibliographical references and index.
Identifiers: LCCN 2022055978 | ISBN 9781032182278 (hardback) | ISBN 9781032182285 (paperback) | ISBN 9781003253501 (ebook)
Subjects: LCSH: Architects and community—United States. | Habitat for Humanity International, Inc.
Classification: LCC NA2543.S6 H56 2023 | DDC 728—dc23/eng/20221209
LC record available at https://lccn.loc.gov/2022055978

ISBN: 978-1-032-18227-8 (hbk)
ISBN: 978-1-032-18228-5 (pbk)
ISBN: 978-1-003-25350-1 (ebk)

DOI: 10.4324/9781003253501

Typeset in Fairfield
by Apex CoVantage, LLC

CONTENTS

x **FOREWORD**
Jonathan Reckford, CEO, Habitat for Humanity International

xiv **PREFACE: NEW DIRECTIONS FOR HABITAT FOR HUMANITY**
David Hinson and Justin Miller

Chapter 1

2 THE IVRV HOUSE

Los Angeles, California

Habitat for Humanity of Greater Los Angeles and Southern California Institute for Architecture

Chapter 2

20 HOUSE OF THE IMMEDIATE FUTURE

Seattle, Washington

Habitat for Humanity Seattle–King County, The Miller Hull Partnership, and Method Homes

Chapter 3

34 STEVENS STREET HOMES

Opelika, Alabama

Auburn Opelika Habitat for Humanity and Auburn University College of Architecture, Design and Construction

Chapter 4

48 EMPOWERHOUSE

Washington, DC

Habitat for Humanity of Washington, DC; Parsons School of Design and Milano School of International Affairs, Management, and Urban Policy at The New School; and Stevens Institute of Technology

Chapter 5

60 SEYMOUR STREET

Middlebury, Vermont

Habitat for Humanity of Addison County, Middlebury College, and McLeod Kredell Architects

Chapter 6

72 BOOTH WOODS

Vergennes, Vermont

Habitat for Humanity of Addison County, Middlebury College, and McLeod Kredell Architects

Chapter 7

82 **GRAND AVENUE DUPLEXES AND BASALT VISTA**

Silt, Colorado

Habitat for Humanity of the Roaring Fork Valley and 2757 design co.

Basalt Vista

Basalt, Colorado

Habitat for Humanity of the Roaring Fork Valley and 2757 design co.

Chapter 8

102 **HABITAT QUINTANA**

San Juan, Puerto Rico

Habitat for Humanity Puerto Rico and Álvarez-Díaz & Villalōn, Architecture & Interior Design

Chapter 9

116 **LOMITA AVENUE TOWNHOMES**

Glendale, California

San Gabriel Valley Habitat for Humanity and [au]workshop architects+urbanists

Chapter 10

132 **MUELLER ROW TOWNHOMES**

Austin, Texas

Austin Habitat for Humanity and Michael Hsu Office of Architecture

Chapter 11

148 **OXFORD GREEN**

Philadelphia, Pennsylvania

Habitat for Humanity Philadelphia and ISA

Chapter 12

164 **SEED AFFORDABLE HOUSING**

Brownsville, Brooklyn, New York

Habitat for Humanity New York City and Westchester County and LATENT Productions

Chapter 13

184   **A CONVERSATION WITH AFFILIATE LEADERS**

199   **Acknowledgments**

203   **References**

207   **Glossary**

211   **Credits**

213   **Index**

FOREWORD

Jonathan Reckford

Chief Executive Officer, Habitat for Humanity International

I have long maintained that at Habitat for Humanity®—and any organization—you have to be religious about your principles but not about your tactics. Situations change, new ideas emerge, and people develop better ways to carry out the mission.

Something as simple as changing a word or phrase can be perceived as upheaval in the beginning, but those decisions become less of a hot button when people have time to live with them for a bit. You will read in the preface to *Designed for Habitat: New Directions for Habitat for Humanity* about the phrase "simple and decent," used by Habitat founder Millard Fuller to describe his vision of the way Habitat houses should be designed and constructed. Millard saw no need for air conditioning, for example. He felt the organization could help keep both construction and utility costs down without it. He saw Habitat's role as building houses that met basic needs for shelter and helped people escape substandard living conditions. Standards change. Almost 50 years later, air conditioning is considered standard, and it makes sense for families purchasing a home to pay slightly more for a second bathroom.

Decades later, people began to question whether "simple" made it sound as if Habitat houses were not well-built structures in which families would be proud to live. Removing that term from our messaging was perceived by many as a significant shift, but it was one that made a huge difference. Today, we describe our work as building safe and affordable homes in partnership with families in need of a decent place to live.

Another instance of change occurred as a result of sundry limitations. Over time, many Habitat affiliates began to add garages or other structural amenities as required by community covenants, for example. Others began to use building materials that were similar to those used in surrounding homes. As the price of land has escalated, building multistory and multifamily homes also became essential.

Making the best use of the housing space and the available lots has led to some interesting new housing designs, as you will see in the following chapters. This has been very exciting for many affiliates, families, and communities. Relatively inexpensive design changes to rooflines and

FOREWORD   xi

porches allowed homes to better fit the neighborhoods—this was intentional, not accidental. However, as housing costs have accelerated far faster than incomes, the principle of keeping costs down is still critical. We have never believed good design has to be more expensive.

Volunteers are the heart of Habitat's work, but they too have come to realize the importance of being flexible. People began to imagine the impact Habitat could make if we focused on the needs of an entire community rather than individual families. Our neighborhood revitalization efforts began to attract groups that could more holistically address neighborhood development. Habitat often initiated conversations and took a seat at the table, but our focus was housing. We invited other people and groups that had different areas of expertise to join the planning and execution of a neighborhood design. That expanded view of our work was reflected when we refreshed our mission statement, which emphasized bringing people together to build homes, communities, and hope.

Habitat's model has always been based on the idea of partnership—but for years, we sought to attract partners that could help us build very standard designs. In the last 10 to 15 years, we have seen how important innovation is if we are to address the global housing crisis. Many of the examples in this book focus on energy-efficient homes and how affiliate leaders engaged with experts to examine new possibilities for building them at scale.

The Stevens Street Homes case study (Chapter 3) from Opelika, Alabama, demonstrates how partnering with other organizations can also help develop, implement, and evaluate house designs that Habitat affiliates alone cannot afford to explore. Auburn Opelika Habitat raised funds equivalent to its traditional house designs, and the Auburn University School of Architecture, Planning, and Landscape Architecture funded the additional costs associated with the elevated energy-saving techniques.

Two years later, affiliate leaders were able to evaluate the cost of investments compared to energy savings. Unlike what we found when we first began to invest in building Energy Star®–rated homes many years ago, the passive building techniques in the Alabama project did not prove to offset the construction costs. But the affiliate—and the broader Habitat family—never would have known that without the university's willingness to underwrite the cost of the design.

I believe we should hit the Pareto optimal point where the purchasing family maximizes its return on energy efficiency. If society wants to invest in going even further (net zero or passive), that financial burden should not fall on low-income families who are already struggling with high costs.

Building more energy-efficient homes that families can afford continues to draw interest, in part, because designing homes that are well ventilated is so critical to health. Studies indicate that those living in homes with good ventilation are less likely to suffer from cardiac and pulmonary ailments that are aggravated by poor indoor air quality.[1] Researchers in the United Kingdom found that mental health is also improved by installation of energy-efficient measures in residential buildings, with tenants reporting that anxiety or depression fell by 50 percent.[2]

So many factors have influenced Habitat's building plans over the years. In areas prone to disasters, emphasis is placed on mitigation. We seek to reduce costs by using the most appropriate and economical building products in various areas of the world. In many locations, we also seek to help families access proper water and sanitation. We also invest in entrepreneurs who have come up with amazing ideas specifically developed to help low-income families around the world build safe homes.

In many places in the United States, a Habitat build site might look much like it did four decades ago—volunteers raising the walls of a single home. In other places, however, one could witness exciting new innovations. Around the world, we are seeing great forward progress as we help more families build a better life.

PREFACE: NEW DIRECTIONS FOR HABITAT FOR HUMANITY

We have been collaborating with Habitat for Humanity® affiliates in Alabama for over 20 years. Our first Habitat project, a design-build studio, was completed in 2002 as a partnership between the architecture program at Auburn University, where we both serve on the faculty, and the Auburn Opelika Habitat affiliate. To prepare for that project—and for the several cycles of collaboration that followed—we began looking for examples of successful partnerships between architects and Habitat for Humanity affiliates from which to learn. That research resulted in our first book, *Designed for Habitat: Collaborations with Habitat for Humanity*, published in 2013.[1]

That book profiled 13 homes developed via partnerships among architects, architecture schools, and Habitat for Humanity affiliates across the United States. The majority of these projects were constructed between 2004 and 2010. As we were interviewing the project teams behind those amazing homes, we could see that Habitat for Humanity's way of thinking about design and about its relationship with design professionals was on the cusp of important changes.

As we wrote *Designed for Habitat: Collaborations with for Habitat for Humanity*, Habitat for Humanity International (HFHI) was in its 35th year. It had become one of the most significant nonprofit affordable housing development organizations in the United States and was active in over 70 countries around the world.

In our first book, we observed that the tensions and conflicts that have surrounded the creation of affordable housing in the United States for decades were almost all present within Habitat for Humanity projects. One of the most tangible examples is balancing the paired goals of building the maximum possible number of homes while creating well-designed and constructed homes that help lift Habitat families out of poverty. Habitat's founder, Millard Fuller, used the phrase "simple and decent" to describe the standard he thought should characterize Habitat homes. He argued that the organization should stand in resistance to the creeping affluence of modern society and build homes that

PREFACE xv

express a "critical perspective towards the market."[2] Habitat affiliates frequently found this approach to be in conflict with their desire to integrate Habitat homes within existing communities, where the form of the then-standard Habitat home—simple, one-story rectangles with low-pitch roofs—was resisted by some communities as incompatible with the image and character of the neighborhoods where Habitat wished to build. In fact, our first collaboration with Habitat (as noted earlier) was initiated as an effort to develop designs that would mesh more sympathetically with existing homes in older Alabama neighborhoods. As we worked through that first partnership, we had firsthand exposure to the tensions between quantity and character in our communications with our partner–client.[3]

A Decade of Challenges and Change

The first decade of the 21st century was a period of intense change within HFHI. Conflicts between Millard Fuller and HFHI's Board of Directors led to Fuller's departure in 2005, in part over disagreements about the future direction of the organization. In 2006, HFHI announced it was moving its leadership offices from Americus, Georgia, the small town where the organization began, to Atlanta—a larger city with greater access to professionals and resources.[4] The COVID-19 pandemic accelerated a trend toward remote work within the organization, further diversifying HFHI's access to professional staff.

As we developed the material for this book 15 years after the events described, we encountered significant shifts within Habitat—both inside the HFHI staff and the affiliates we interviewed—regarding the way it viewed its role within respective communities and within the larger ecosphere of affordable housing development.

Mitigating the Impacts of Climate Change

Our discussions with HFHI staff suggest that a series of natural and economic disasters occurring in this decade were also significant catalysts for reflection and change for the organization.[5] The impact of Hurricane Katrina in 2005—one of the most devastating natural disasters in modern US history—along with subsequent cycles of natural disasters that have followed pushed HFHI leadership to explore strategies for incorporating resilience into its standards for construction in hazard-prone regions. Rising energy costs and the resulting impact on low-income families led to energy-related improvements in construction approaches shifting to the center of HFHI's affiliate education efforts. The initiatives were further supported by dialogue between HFHI's US team and the staff leading the organization's growing international initiatives regarding the disproportionate impact of climate change on the families it serves. In 2022, HFHI issued a formal statement regarding housing and climate change, challenging itself to "build stronger, more disaster-resilient and more energy-efficient housing" and to increase the "use of sustainable natural resources and construction practices while reducing the emission of greenhouse gasses throughout a home's lifecycle."[6]

The housing collapse that followed the economic crisis of 2008 also prompted a cycle of reflection on how to make Habitat homes more resilient in the face of housing market volatility—ultimately leading HFHI to identify investments in energy efficiency and hazard resilience as keys to providing "long-term affordability" to its partner families.

HFHI has utilized corporate partnerships—in particular, ties to building product manufacturers—as a source of financial support and in-kind material donations from the early stages of its emergence as a nationally recognized affordable housing advocate. Coming out of the housing market crisis of 2009 to 2011, HFHI staff and several corporate partners saw these partnerships as a means not just to support change within Habitat but to drive change within the affordable housing sector.

Leveraging several significant incentive funding and material donation programs, HFHI leadership sought to make homeowners less vulnerable to rising energy costs by encouraging Habitat affiliates to make improvements in energy efficiency. Perhaps the most significant example of this type of program was the Home Depot Foundation's Partners in Sustainable Building program, which began in 2009 and provided $30 million to support construction of Habitat homes that met the Energy Star® guidelines.[7] In turn, these programs generated a demand surge for the other essential components of an energy-focused housing ecosphere: from the building products and equipment needed to achieve the standards to the network of independent raters and inspectors needed to provide the incentives' certifications.

While affiliate building practices tend to slip back to their pre-incentive norms when the extra funding goes away, the incremental change has been significant. One benefit of these programs has been the innovation sparked within individual affiliates as they sought out the most cost-effective way to achieve the incentivized outcomes.

Examples of this innovation are found in several case studies featured here, including the Stevens Street Homes (Chapter 3) and Empowerhouse (Chapter 4), which incorporated Passive House standards, and the Basalt Vista project (Chapter 7), which leveraged local incentives to create a community of near–net-zero homes.

Innovation from the Bottom Up

When we first began researching HFHI's influence on affiliates, its construction standards—covering everything from the size of Habitat homes to the materials used to construct them—were administered in a very "top-down" way.[8] That culture underwent significant change.

While the construction staff at HFHI still develop national construction standards, these are much more closely tied to innovations incubated at the affiliate level. Once an improvement in building approach has been broadly tested and evaluated, that new approach is shared across the Habitat affiliate community with support from the HFHI staff. The most impactful of these innovations eventually become part of HFHI's national standards. For example, Energy Star® certification, incentivized via the Home Depot Foundation grant beginning in 2009, will become a required standard for all Habitat homes in 2024.

Embracing Design Innovation

This shift from top-down to bottom-up influence can also be seen in the approach to home design. When we initiated our first collaboration with Habitat in 2001, we were given a blue three-ring binder containing floor plans and product specifications developed by the HFHI construction team based in Americus. Those designs were widely adopted by affiliates and became the image of a "Habitat home" in the eyes of many. While many affiliates still build homes following that design approach, we encountered significantly more diversity in the design approaches adopted by affiliates as we researched examples for this book. HFHI staff now administer an annual design awards program to recognize exemplary projects developed by affiliates. These designs, among others, are made available for use by other affiliates via an online plan library. Oxford Green (Chapter 11) and Basalt Vista (Chapter 7) have won awards in this program.

Several factors underpin the shift in design thinking within the national organization and local affiliates, but none seems more significant than the desire to more closely integrate Habitat homes into existing mixed-income neighborhoods. In *Designed for Habitat: New Directions for Habitat for Humanity*, we studied several examples of homes, such as Project 1800 and Webster Street, designed to fit into sites within established neighborhoods and blend as seamlessly as possible with the aesthetic of the surrounding context.[9] Several of the projects profiled here, including the Lomita Avenue Townhomes (Chapter 9) and Oxford Green (Chapter 11), illustrate this design response.

PREFACE   xix

Embracing New Partners

We also encountered a growing desire by local affiliates to partner with for-profit developers to integrate Habitat projects within new market-rate housing developments. Often involving sites developed as public–private partnerships between local communities or public housing authorities and private developers, these projects leverage the requirement to integrate affordable housing into the overall development plan in order to open sites for Habitat homes that would otherwise be too expensive for the affiliate to acquire. Mueller Row (Chapter 10) and Oxford Green (Chapter 11) illustrate Habitat developments that fall within larger, mixed-income development sites.

Changing Scale

The single-family, one-story home on its own lot is the predominant pattern for Habitat homes across the United States. However, Habitat affiliates working in cities with older, high-density development patterns, such as Philadelphia's iconic row house neighborhoods and Brooklyn's multistory walk-ups, have been building homes that match the type and scale of homes endemic to their location for decades. However, rising land costs have forced affiliates such as Austin, Seattle, and Roaring Fork—which were formerly accustomed to building the single-family detached home model—to adopt housing solutions that result in more units per acre. Our discussions with Habitat San Gabriel Valley (Lomita Avenue Townhomes, Chapter 9) and Habitat Austin (Mueller Row, Chapter 10) revealed that multifamily design solutions are the only way the affiliate can approach sites closer to city centers with access to public transportation and social services. These affiliates still build single-family homes in more distant suburban communities, but client families opting for those sites are much more reliant on personal automobiles and face longer work commutes.

Habitat affiliates across the United States are exploring ways to develop more units per square foot through accessory dwelling units, duplexes, townhomes, and midrise blocks. Nine of the 12 projects in this book illustrate these housing typologies. Affiliates are also leveraging changes to zoning regulations to develop single-family detached homes in developments with little or no private yards but a larger shared open space.

Another side effect of this push into higher-density home configurations is increased engagement between Habitat affiliates and licensed design professionals. In most areas of the United States, single-family detached homes do not require the involvement of licensed architects. In many areas, this includes duplex homes. Consequently, architects are only involved in a very small percentage of this sector of the housing market.[10] However, multifamily home typologies (and some high-density neighborhood schemes) push the projects into the realm where building regulations require the involvement of licensed design professionals. An affiliate's first multifamily project may likely be its first experience with an architect. On the other side of the team, the partnership with a Habitat affiliate may be the architect's first experience with a project where the budget constraints are so challenging. The challenge of calibrating design aspirations to fit the affiliate's budget was a recurring topic in our interviews with project teams for this book.

These development typologies present a significant challenge to Habitat's core value of building homes with community volunteers working alongside the future homeowner families. Higher-density development almost always means taller buildings and more complex construction details—conditions far less favorable to unskilled volunteer builders than the one-story, relatively simple building at the core of Habitat's delivery model. As was the case for many of the larger projects profiled here, the financing arrangements underpinning larger projects tend to come with set timeframes in which to complete units. The stories behind each chapter reveal that affiliate leaders are caught between the schedule and efficiency benefits of building with skilled (and paid) subcontractors and the community-building impact of the volunteer-centered approach. As we discussed this issue with affiliate leaders, we encountered a strong commitment to the traditional Habitat volunteer model coupled with creativity as to how and where the volunteering occurred. Some affiliates designate specific sites as their "volunteer sites" while leaning more heavily on paid subcontractors where schedule constraints are tight. In one of the most interesting examples of how affiliates are shifting the focus of volunteers, we heard an affiliate explain that it used professional framers for the schedule advantage but focused volunteers on the task of air sealing—a critical building performance booster that they could easily complete.

The increasing scale of Habitat projects has also presented affiliates with challenges in financing the construction costs of projects prior to selling the units to homeowner families. For the Oxford Green project (Chapter 11), Habitat Philadelphia had to raise $7 million to cover the anticipated construction costs before the Philadelphia Housing Authority could transfer the property to the affiliate. For the SEED project (Chapter 12), Habitat New York City established a partnership with the State of New York Mortgage Agency to help access the $29 million in financing needed to build the project. "We would never have been able to do [the SEED project] if we'd had to use the traditional Habitat financing model. That's an important part of how we've adapted the Habitat model to get to this scale of development," observed Karen Haycox, chief executive officer of Habitat for Humanity New York City and Westchester County. In 2017, HFHI initiated a new program called Habitat Mortgage Solutions designed to help affiliates with the financial services and capital needed to tackle the larger-scale development now becoming more commonplace across the Habitat network.[11]

Advocating for Policy Change

"We realize that we can't do it all ourselves," said Adrienne Goolsby, HFHI's senior vice president of the United States and Canada. "Habitat has to partner with others, both on a local level and a national level, to really address housing affordability more broadly."[12]

Conversations with the HFHI staff, as well as with local affiliate leaders, highlight another significant shift from the early decades of Habitat: embracing the task of influencing local and national public policy regarding affordable housing development. This involves advocacy on topics such as regulations that impact where affordable housing can be developed as well as increased public incentives to support the incorporation of climate resilience into affordable housing. It also involves advocacy for public financing options that increase the affiliates' capacity to scale up affordable housing development activity. For example, Habitat Austin spent over a year working with the City of Austin to increase the number of allowable affordable home units on parcels, ultimately leading the city to create a new program called Affordability Unlocked, which has proven to be a big boost to affordable housing development.[13]

Conclusion

It has been nearly 50 years since Habitat for Humanity began its "partnership housing" model in Americus, Georgia. The organization is active in all 50 states in the United States and in more than 70 countries around the world. Established in 1976, Habitat for Humanity began its work at a time when public financing for affordable housing in the United States was evaporating after the federal programs were suspended in 1973.[14] The focus of affordable housing development shifted from the public sector to the nonprofit sector, where it has remained—at least for the United States. Those who want to impact the supply or the quality of affordable housing in this country are going to do it with a nonprofit partner like Habitat.

With more than 2,100 active affiliates and 39 million people served, it would be hard to overstate Habitat's impact on affordable housing development over the last five decades. As longtime observers and partners with the organization, we are even more impressed with the way the organization is adapting and evolving to meet the momentous challenges of housing affordability in the age of climate change. As this book illustrates, this includes creative adaptation and evolution in the way Habitat affiliates and their partners approach design and construction. We hope you find these projects as inspiring as we do.

Chapter 1

The IVRV House

Los Angeles, California
Habitat for Humanity® of Greater Los Angeles and Southern California Institute for Architecture

Key Partnerships

Darin Johnstone (Faculty Lead) and Howard Chen (Student Lead), SCI-Arc
Darrell Simien (Senior Vice President for Community Development) and Robert Dwelle (Director of Housing Development and Design), Habitat for Humanity of Greater Los Angeles

Program Summary

Suburban neighborhood context
3-bedroom, 2.5-bath, single-family detached home
1,200 square feet

Project Overview

The IVRV House was a collaboration between Habitat for Humanity of Greater Los Angeles (Habitat LA) and the Southern California Institute for Architecture, a renowned design school in Los Angeles known as SCI-Arc. Driven by student teams, the home provided an opportunity for students to explore affordable housing design and to see their research realized as a family home—and for the Habitat affiliate to gain a better understanding of the possibilities that come with academic partnerships.[1]

DOI: 10.4324/9781003253501-1

Catalysts for Collaboration

In early 2014, Los Angeles County Supervisor Mark Ridley Thomas's office reached out to Habitat for Humanity Greater Los Angeles (Habitat LA) to offer funding support and a site donation in the West Athens neighborhood of Los Angeles. The County believed that innovation in housing design could act as a catalyst for revitalization in the area and suggested that Habitat LA could partner with SCI-Arc on the design of a house that would draw positive attention to the neighborhood and serve as a catalyst for new housing investment in the area.

Darrell Simien, Senior Vice President for Community Development for Habitat LA, knew little about SCI-Arc beyond the school's high standing within the professional community and reputation for avant-garde design. While Habitat LA had no prior experience collaborating with an architecture school, they were excited by the chance to see what the students could do. "We pride ourselves for being ahead of the curve and trying on new ideas," Simien said. "Any time we get the opportunity to get outside help that might improve our product, we're going to check it out."

Simien and Robert Dwelle, Habitat LA's Director of Housing Development and Design, met with John Enright, SCI-Arc's Undergraduate Program Chair at the time, and Darin Johnstone, a SCI-Arc faculty member, to develop a process for the collaboration. Enright and Johnstone mapped out a plan whereby SCI-Arc students would be involved in the project through multisemester studios and stay involved in the construction via a series of seminars. The first studio would develop multiple options, and the subsequent studio would refine the selected design and develop construction documents for the house. Habitat LA would be responsible for raising funds for the base house, and SCI-Arc would help raise funds for design innovation, including the components of the design essential to the sustainability goals of the project.

Design Process

In the fall term of 2014, the first group of 20 graduate and undergraduate architecture students researched evolving trends in housing, how principles of sustainability could be integrated into affordable housing, and how construction systems impacted design at a single-family residential scale.

Building on this research phase, the students worked in teams on the development of design proposals tailored to the project site and a range of prototypical family scenarios—two parents with two children, a single parent with two children, multigenerational families, and so on. Simien and Dwelle visited with the student teams several times over the course of the term, briefing the students on the affiliate's approach to housing design and construction and providing feedback on the students' research and evolving design proposals.

As the design studio progressed, Johnstone and the SCI-Arc students were committed to rethinking affordable housing from the ground up. Reflecting on this process, Dwelle observed, "It took some honing to get the designs down to something we could build, but it was really amazing to see their work." Johnstone viewed this stage as a key part of the student experience—where the goals and agendas of Habitat LA, and those of the SCI-Arc faculty and students, were sorted out.

At the conclusion of the fall studio, a panel of SCI-Arc faculty, practicing architects, and representatives from Habitat LA and the LA County Supervisor's office reviewed five student design proposals. The selected design, nicknamed the "InVerse-ReVerse house" (IVRV) by the students, evolved from a simple extrusion of a two-story gable form and was chosen for its iconic association with the traditional form of homes in the area. The gable form extended to cover two parking spaces on the first level, which were required by local zoning regulations. Then, a series of alterations challenged the building envelope to perform differently than expected.

On the south elevation of the IVRV House, the windows were inset deeply to provide shading. On the north elevation, the street-facing roof was cut to allow light into the balcony, bedroom, and entry courtyard. The entry courtyard, which flanked the parking space at the front half of the first level, featured an innovative "eco-screen," designed to shade the courtyard and hold the house's future photovoltaic panels. The trellis also incorporated vinyl strips painted with a photocatalytic coating to capture and neutralize harmful particles in the air. The initial configuration of the selected design also included an accessory dwelling unit connected to the main structure by a bridge on the second level.

In the second phase of the design process that began in the spring of 2015, Johnstone led a team of new and continuing students through design refinement; budget reconciliation, which eliminated the accessory unit; construction documentation; and permit applications. The students worked with consulting engineers to detail the building's structure and integrate mechanical, electrical, and plumbing systems. This team of students also participated in meetings with the local community and building officials as the project moved through the permitting process. Johnstone tapped one of the students, Howard Chen, to act as coordinator of the student teams.

Near the end of the second stage of the project, Habitat LA selected the homeowner family—an Army veteran, his wife, and two children. While the students had hoped for homeowner involvement earlier in the process, bringing the future homeowners onboard invigorated the project team. "The clients gave the project life, and they became such champions and advocates for the project. They really loved it," Johnstone said.

Construction Process

As Habitat LA bid out the subcontracted portions of the project, the funds raised by Habitat LA and SCI-Arc fell short of the cost to build the project. The LA County Supervisor's office stepped in with the funding needed to close the gap, and construction began in the summer of 2015.

The IVRV House's unique design translated into new lessons and challenges for both the students and Habitat LA as the construction process began. While the students had developed very detailed construction drawings, these drawings presumed a level of accuracy that was hard to achieve in the field. The angles and tolerances in the student's construction details forced the construction team to adopt a slower, more careful approach, which created some friction on the job site.

"Our staff and long-time volunteers were used to a more conventional design, where you put siding up and knock it out in a day," Dwelle said. "The precision required on this house was much greater than what we'd built before. Some of our team enjoyed the challenge of tackling something different, but some just wanted to nail a box together." This conflict could have derailed the project, but according to Simien and Dwelle, several factors ensured that the house was constructed with a high degree of fidelity to the original design.

The first of these was the involvement of the SCI-Arc students during construction. They were onsite once a week throughout the construction phase. Chen, the student team leader, advocated for the authenticity of the design and adapted details based on feedback from the construction team. "I just can't express how impressed we were with him," Dwelle remarked.

The homeowners' passion and commitment to the design and sustainability initiatives also helped keep the project on track. Regularly onsite, the family was committed to seeing the project built the way the students intended. Even the youngest daughter, who was only five or six at the time, showed dedication to her new home, leading tours of the project during construction. After watching the fundraising videos, she could walk through the framing, pointing out each room. "She nicknamed the house 'Noah's Ark' because the project looks a bit like a big ship," Johnstone said. "The homeowners speak so beautifully and poetically about the project and what it means to them. It's really powerful."

Lastly, the LA County Supervisor's support pushed the project to realization. Supervisor Thomas was an enthusiastic advocate for the project, helping keep Habitat LA and SCI-Arc leadership aligned with the efforts of Johnstone, Simien, and the project team. This external advocacy for the project was especially critical within Habitat LA. "If it had just been me and Rob pushing this project, it would never have happened," Simien stated.

The whole team developed pride and a sense of accomplishment in the project as it took shape. "To be part of it was special," he said. "In the end it was a win-win for everyone, for us, for the family, for the neighborhood, and for SCI-Arc."

Key Lessons

Both sides of this collaboration learned from each other and gained a better appreciation of the other's expertise. "I had a series of preconceptions about Habitat that were just not correct," Johnstone said. "Once you understand their model, it's easy to understand how to work within their constraints."

While acknowledging that integrating a design-build studio into an architecture curriculum was challenging, Johnstone noted that the results were worth the effort. He commended the impact that the project had on the students and its potential influence on their trajectories into future architecture practices.

From Johnstone's perspective, the most important aspect of SCI-Arc's approach to the project was their emphasis on research. The students embraced the exploration of how affordable housing could be reimagined, and those investigations "indelibly shaped the outcome," he said. He recommended a research-focused approach to any architecture faculty considering a nonprofit collaboration.

The IVRV house gave Habitat LA the opportunity to explore how the affiliate could approach design in the future. "We can't keep building the same box forever," Simien said. "We're always looking for ways to have a bigger impact for our homeowner families."

The forward-thinking collaboration has already translated into tangible benefits for Habitat LA. Since this project was completed in 2016, many of the energy-conservation strategies of the IVRV house have become building code mandates in Los Angeles. Despite the growing pains of the affiliate's first collaboration, the partnership with SCI-Arc helped Habitat LA understand how to work more effectively with professional architects. "We have great relationships with several large architecture firms now," Simien said. "We lean on them to help us make our homes better."

THE IVRV HOUSE   7

IVRV House site plan

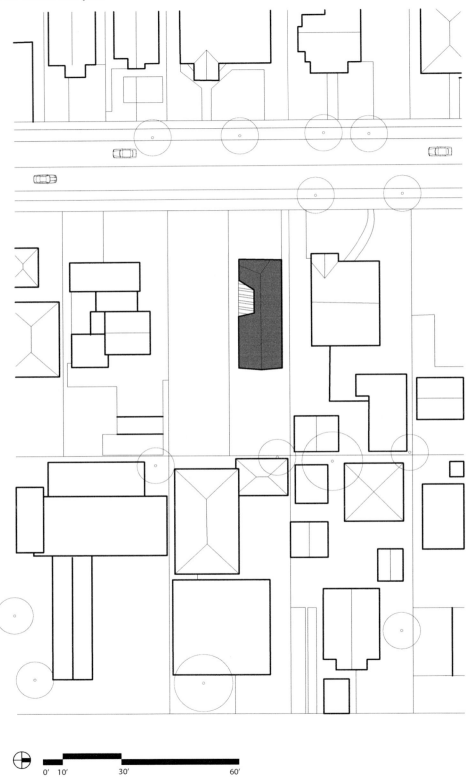

0' 10'   30'   60'

8   THE IVRV HOUSE

IVRV House floor plans

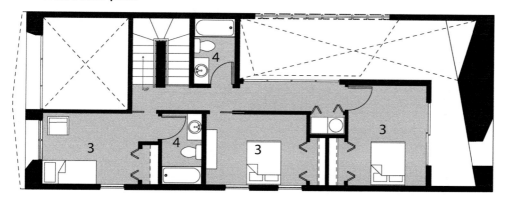

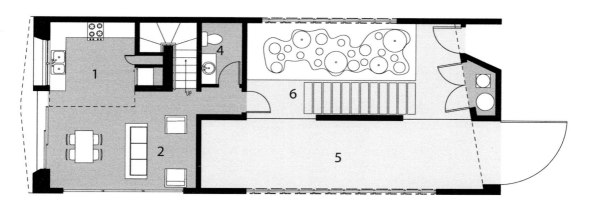

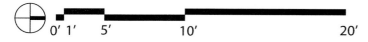

1 Kitchen
2 Living Room
3 Bedroom
4 Bathroom
5 Carport
6 Entry Court

View from the street

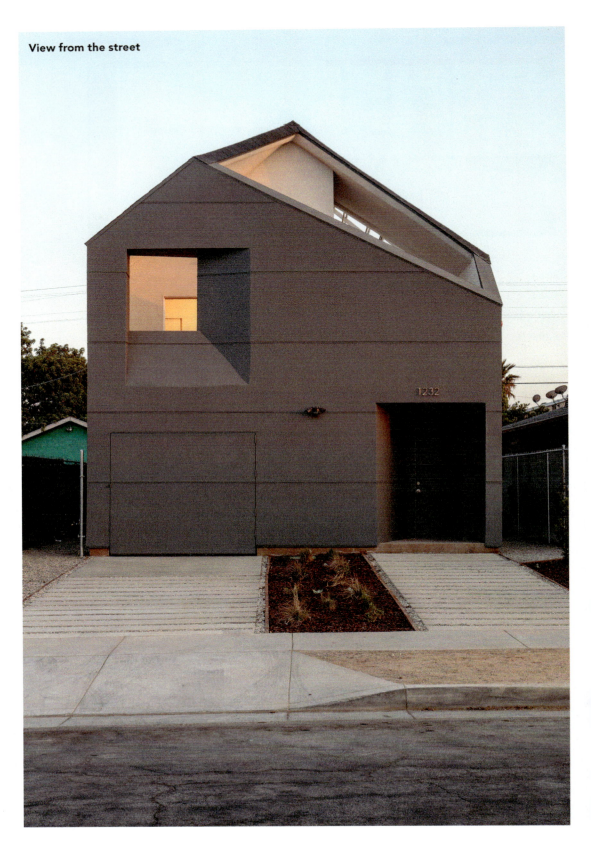

10 THE IVRV HOUSE

View from rear

View of the entry courtyard and garage

View of the kitchen and entry foyer

View of the kitchen and stairs

View of stairs from the upper level corridor

THE IVRV HOUSE 19

Chapter 2

House of the Immediate Future

Seattle, Washington

Habitat for Humanity® Seattle–King County, The Miller Hull Partnership, and Method Homes

Key Partnerships

Marty Kooistra (Executive Director), Habitat for Humanity Seattle–King County

Mike Jobes (Design Principal), The Miller Hull Partnership

Brian Abramson (CEO), Method Homes

Program Summary

Demonstration home prototype

4-bedroom, 2-bath single-family detached home

1,360 square feet

Project Overview

The House of the Immediate Future (HOIF) was a collaboration between Habitat for Humanity Seattle–King County; Miller Hull, a Seattle-based architecture firm that specializes in environmentally sensitive design; and Method Homes, a modular housing prefabrication company. Initiated for the Seattle Center Next 50 celebration, the home's innovation and collaboration were driven by the Habitat affiliate, and they push the envelope in terms of performance and flexibility—particularly in the home's ability to be deconstructed and reassembled. The house was built twice, once on the grounds of the Seattle Center for the Next 50 celebration and finally in Seattle for a Habitat for Humanity partner family.[1]

DOI: 10.4324/9781003253501-2

Catalysts for Collaboration

In 1962, Seattle hosted the World's Fair. Seattle's fair provided an opportunity to transform the city but also to look ahead and speculate about the future. One of these speculations was an exhibition house—the House of the Future.

In 2012, Seattle hosted Next 50 at the Seattle Center, celebrating the 50th anniversary of the fair. As planning for the Seattle Center Next 50 celebration began, the steering committee revisited the House of the Future as one of the exhibitions of the celebration. Ron Rochon, a partner at Miller Hull, a Seattle-based design firm specializing in customized and sustainable design and member of the Next 50 steering committee, contacted the Seattle Habitat affiliate to collaborate and showcase the organization's work in affordable housing, building the House of the Immediate Future (HOIF) as part of the anniversary exhibition.

Habitat for Humanity Seattle–King County CEO Marty Kooistra saw this as an opportunity to educate the public about the organization's local and international work. Kooistra proposed that two demonstration structures be constructed: a Habitat for Humanity International house that would be representative of the construction techniques and house sizes built in international settings and a house for a prospective homeowner. Envisioned as the HOIF, the homeowner's house utilized "reasonably attainable technology" and building methods, ambitious energy conservation and generation strategies, built-in adaptability, and an ability to be reassembled on a permanent site following the Seattle Next 50 exhibition. Kooistra wanted the house to "be a prototype: to test a new approach to the integration of modular construction, internal layout flexibility, multigenerational housing, aging in place, and work-from-home scenarios."

Design Process

With Kooistra and the affiliate's participation, Miller Hull committed to the design work as a pro bono service. Mike Jobes led the design team and helped develop the framework of the design brief through a series of micro conferences involving regional sustainability experts, construction supervisors, and affiliate leadership and field construction leaders. These micro conferences identified strategies and technologies that allowed the team to address the client's goals. The house was a prototype investigating enhanced building performance, project delivery methods, and spatial adaptability. The prototype tested net-zero readiness and modular construction within the parameters of a Habitat home.

The micro conferences prompted the team to lean heavily into prefabrication, which led Miller Hull to add Method Homes, a local modular housing prefabrication company, to the design team. The final team included key members from the affiliate's leadership and a field construction director, the Miller Hull design team, and the fabrication team at Method Homes.

The relocation of the house following the exhibition provided the immediate and most obvious challenge, and the team had to determine ways to involve volunteers in the construction process of a house that would be assembled, disassembled, and reassembled on a different site.

As a response to these challenges, the team mixed prefabrication methods that involved modular construction with onsite construction that maximized volunteer hours. The house was built with a modular "smart core" that contained the plumbing, electrical, and mechanical systems, including a photovoltaic array and a cistern for captured rainwater. This central core localized the systems in two compact volumes that could be set with a small crane and completed with work from specialized trades.

The volunteers assembled a panelized double-stud wall that enclosed the rooms adjacent to the core modules. This high-performance double-stud wall simplified construction, minimized thermal bridging, and provided additional insulation for increased energy efficiency. This site-fabricated envelope allowed for easy assembly and reassembly. While other assembly methods may have been easier, the team "did not want the idea of moving the home to detract from replicability," Jobes said.

The team designed the floor plan to anticipate household changes—such as multigenerational families, a need to work from home, and families aging in place. The prototype needed the flexibility to be configured as a detached single-family house, as a duplex, or in a townhouse configuration that stretched the width of the floor plan. On the ground floor, the modular core separated the living area from the private rooms of the house. The interior walls carried no structural load and could be reconfigured, allowing the house to adapt to residents' changing needs. In addition to overall dimensions, the team studied window placement to allow for this potential variation. The design team consulted the homeowners—a family of five—to decide on the final configuration of the home.

As the design work progressed, the team identified the ultimate site for the house. Dwell Development, a Seattle-based residential builder focused on sustainable development and construction, donated a parcel at the Rainier Vista development—42 environmentally conscious, transit-oriented homes in the Columbia City neighborhood of Seattle. The team worked to align the design with the Rainier Vista guidelines, which helped them select the color palette. The team identified a rainscreen system consisting of a mix of reclaimed wood and cementitious panels for the cladding.

Construction Process

The initial site of the HOIF was in a parking lot on the grounds of the Seattle Center at the base of the Space Needle as part of the Seattle Next 50 centennial celebration.

Habitat Seattle–King County began construction on both the HOIF and a "World House" as part of the exhibition; the location provided a large staging area for both houses. Method Homes coordinated with site leaders and specialized trades to begin fabrication of the HOIF's wet core modules offsite in the Method Homes fabrication facility. Brian Abramson, the

CEO of Method Homes, recalled the value of having the affiliate's site leads in the factory to make sure the team was in sync.

The particular mix of offsite prefabrication and onsite construction necessitated clear and continuous communication, not only among the team but also with inspectors on- and offsite. While the modules were being fabricated, Habitat Seattle–King County organized materials and choreographed wall panel assembly methods for volunteers. In the Method Homes fabrication facility, the team was also able to coordinate the vertical connections for mechanical, electrical, and plumbing systems before the two modules were stacked onsite.

Sellen Construction, a Seattle-based construction company that partnered frequently with the affiliate, assisted with this process by precutting all the dimensional lumber—which had been donated by Weyerhaeuser—to the correct dimensions for the wall panels that would make up the double-stud wall system. The double-stud wall system required two sets of panels—an exterior and interior set. The exterior panels were assembled first, while the house was framed and dried in. Then, volunteers assembled the interior panels. Jobes recalled that the interior panel framing occurred inside, which kept the interior panels and partitions dry as well as dimensionally stable and later made finish work much easier. The interior panels were joined to the exterior panels at a 2×12–inch baseplate and header, forming a single wall panel. While work moved forward on the interior, the team installed the cementitious panel cladding systems and an exterior rainscreen, which consisted of boards reclaimed from a barn prior to its demolition. Overall, materials were selected for their durability and ease of maintenance, installation, and removal. As Jobes described, the cementitious panel's stainless steel clips were easy to secure through the sheathing and provided a simple installation method by allowing the panel to rest on the clips and be secured at the top. Designed for maintenance or easy replacement of a single panel, this installation proved to be a volunteer-friendly way to clad the building and made disassembly relatively easy.

Not everything was installed at the Seattle Center site. However, this turned into a blessing in disguise, as the disassembly process was more complex than anticipated. During disassembly, the Habitat Seattle–King County job site supervisor cataloged every piece of the house, storing and then retrieving them for reassembly in Rainier Vista. Aiming to keep the pieces as large as possible for a quicker installation at the final site, the walls were disassembled to the double-stud wall panel. In preparation for the reassembly, the team constructed the foundations and ground floor slab at the new site. Abramson said the radiant floor system and connection to the modules was one of the more challenging aspects of the reassembly process, but once complete, the larger wall panels made the rest of the assembly process move quickly. This left less framing for volunteers to do, but it meant that they were more involved in installing the air and water barriers and rainscreen cladding system that contributed to the home's long-term energy performance.

The move to Rainier Vista saw some changes to the original design. The rainwater cistern and the solar panels were not installed due to cost constraints. However, the air sealing and robust assembly R-values allowed for a relatively small mechanical system for the home. As a net-zero–ready home, the HOIF was one of the most energy-efficient houses that the affiliate had completed. As all the team members pointed out, there were compelling spatial gains as a result of the energy and construction goals. The double-stud wall was deep enough to bounce daylight off the jambs and sills and provide a window seat.

Key Lessons

By all accounts, the HOIF was a successful collaboration. All of the partners pointed to clear communication and consistency—both on- and offsite—throughout the project as key to completing the project—twice.

As a test case for modular construction and prefabrication, the partners left the project with different takeaways. Habitat for Humanity Seattle–King County is not actively incorporating modular construction in their work, while Method Homes is advancing the model of a mixed modular—utility core—and panelized prefabrication project delivery. Jobes described the lessons that Miller Hull learned regarding prefabrication and residential energy as impactful. Miller Hull expressed excitement about future collaborations with the affiliate that have opportunities to make an impact on both the building industry and those it houses. Kooistra has carried lessons and enthusiasm about these specific issues of scalability and pace of change forward into his current role as Executive Director at the Seattle-based Housing Development Consortium.

HOIF site plan

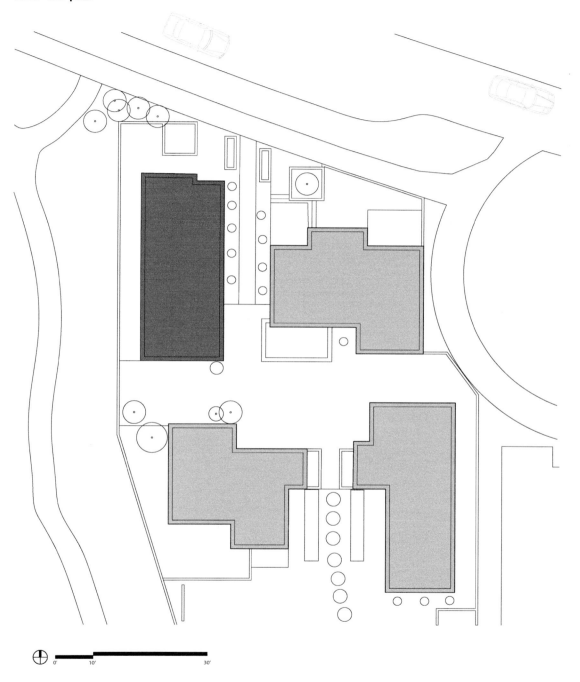

HOUSE OF THE IMMEDIATE FUTURE

HOIF floor plans

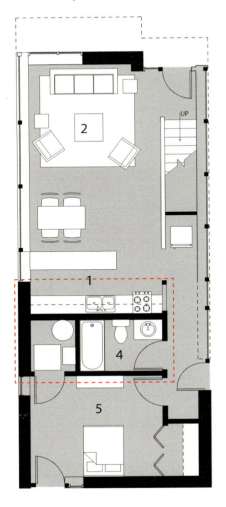
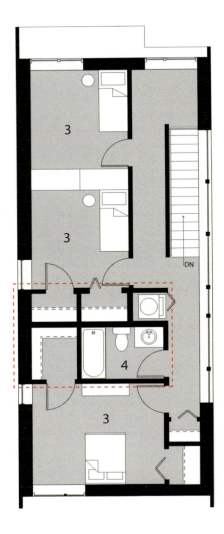

1 Kitchen
2 Living Room
3 Bedroom
4 Bathroom
5 Flex Room
⌐ ⌐ Prefabricated Wet Core

View of east facade installed at the exhibition site

View of west facade installed at the Seattle Center Next 50 celebration site

Diagram of key building components

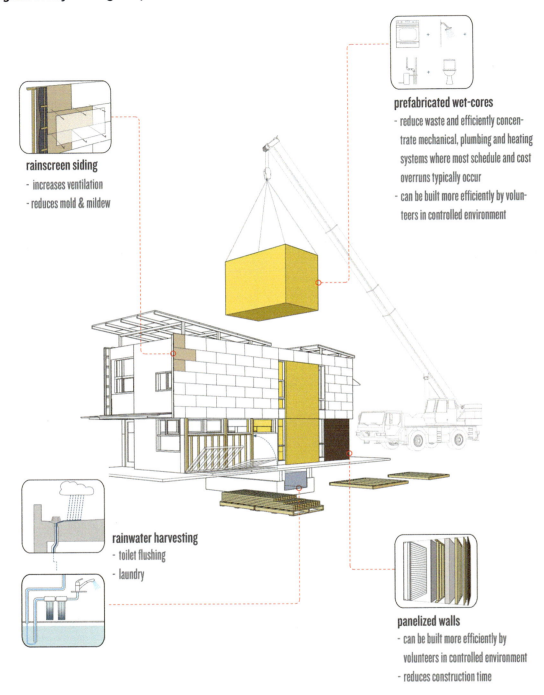

prefabricated wet-cores
- reduce waste and efficiently concentrate mechanical, plumbing and heating systems where most schedule and cost overruns typically occur
- can be built more efficiently by volunteers in controlled environment

rainscreen siding
- increases ventilation
- reduces mold & mildew

rainwater harvesting
- toilet flushing
- laundry

panelized walls
- can be built more efficiently by volunteers in controlled environment
- reduces construction time

HOUSE OF THE IMMEDIATE FUTURE
MILLER HULL
ARCHITECTURE & PLANNING
SYSTEMS

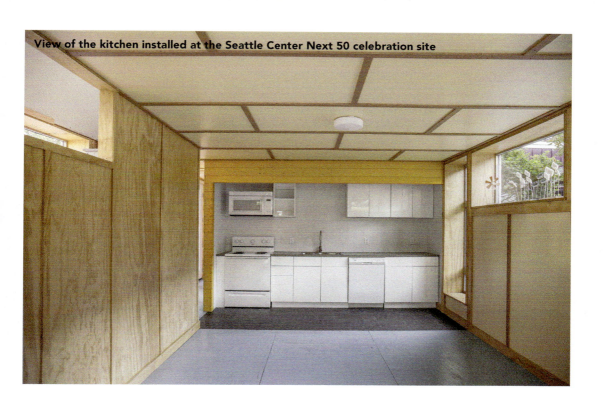
View of the kitchen installed at the Seattle Center Next 50 celebration site

View of the entrance and east facade at the permanent site

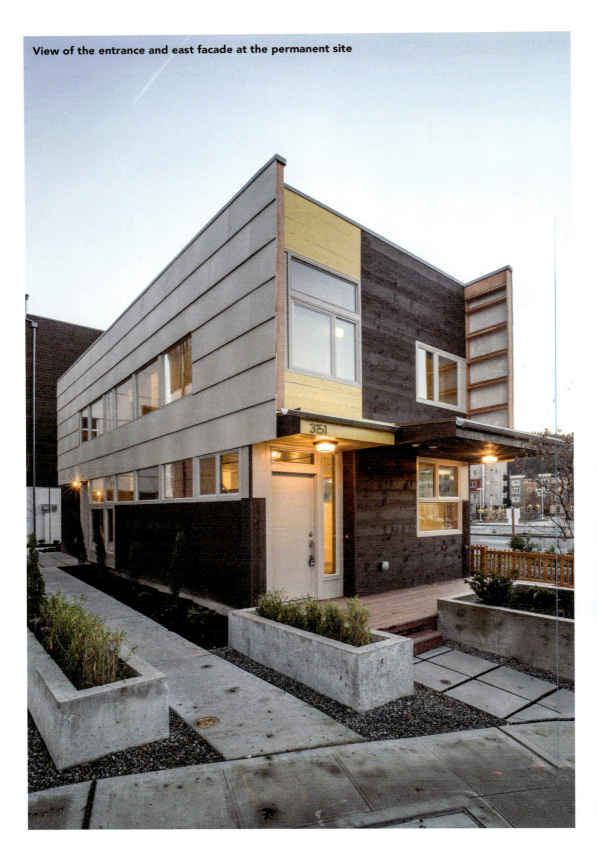

View of the entrance and west facade at the permanent site

Chapter 3

Stevens Street Homes

Opelika, Alabama

Auburn Opelika Habitat for Humanity® and Auburn University College of Architecture, Design and Construction

Key Partnerships

Mark Grantham (Executive Director), Auburn Opelika Habitat for Humanity

David Hinson (Professor), Auburn University School of Architecture, Planning and Landscape Architecture

Mike Hosey (Lecturer and Field Lab Manager), Auburn University McWhorter School of Building Science

Program Summary

Suburban neighborhood context

Two single-family detached houses

2-bedroom, 1-bath homes

912 square feet

Project Overview

The two homes on Stevens Street in Opelika, Alabama, were built over two consecutive years via design-build studios and community service classes in the College of Architecture, Design and Construction at Auburn University. The two homes are identical plans and are built two doors apart on a suburban street. The first home (House 66) was built to meet the requirements of the Phius certification standard, and the second home (House 68) was built to the US Department of Energy's Zero Energy Ready Home (Zero Ready) standard. A team of research faculty at Auburn monitored post occupancy energy use on both homes to compare the cost of construction and cost of operation associated with the two homes.[1]

DOI: 10.4324/9781003253501-3

Catalysts for Collaboration

The partnership between Auburn Opelika Habitat for Humanity (AO Habitat) and the College of Architecture, Design and Construction (Auburn) began in 2001 and has produced several cycles of design research and award-winning homes produced via design-build studios within the architecture program.[2] The architecture program at Auburn is also home to the Rural Studio, one of the leading design-build teaching programs in the United States.

Since 2004, the Rural Studio has pursued an initiative focused on housing affordability, known as the 20K Home program, which has generated dozens of homes designed and constructed by teams of Auburn students. In 2016, the Rural Studio launched the Front Porch Initiative to focus on partnerships with affordable housing advocacy groups beyond its three-county service area in western Alabama.

Each round of collaboration between AO Habitat and Auburn included improved energy performance as an objective. The partnership produced the first Energy Star®-certified Habitat for Humanity home in Alabama (2002), and Auburn faculty had worked with Habitat affiliates across the state to help them adopt improved energy performance goals.[3] In the spring and summer of 2017, Auburn faculty member David Hinson and AO Habitat Executive Director Mark Grantham met to begin planning a design-build studio. The collaboration would utilize one of the Front Porch Initiative's "product line" home prototypes modified to elevate the home's performance to an ultrahigh-efficiency standard with the goal of understanding how the cost of investment in energy performance would compare to the costs saved by reduced energy use.

Following the pattern adopted on previous research-centered collaborations, AO Habitat committed to funding the project at a level comparable to its typical new home projects, and the Auburn team agreed to fund the additional costs associated with the elevated performance goals through grants and in-kind donations.

Grantham and Hinson selected the Buster's House prototype from the Front Porch Initiative's product line.[4] The prototype worked well with the affiliate's need for a small, two-bedroom home and the constraints of the pie-shaped, narrow lots that the affiliate owned on Stevens Street. Initially, the Buster's House design had been developed and constructed by a Rural Studio student team in 2017.

Hinson proposed to construct the first home, known as House 66 to AO Habitat, to the Phius standard and install monitoring equipment in the home to enable post occupancy energy use monitoring. Following the completion of the first home in 2018, AO Habitat and Auburn agreed to build a second version of the same design two doors down from the first home (House 68). This time, the design was adapted to meet the requirements of the Zero Ready standard and monitored with the same equipment. This side-by-side comparison allowed the team to study the cost of construction and the energy use across the two homes.

Design Process

Since Buster's House was a predesigned prototype, Hinson and the student teams involved in the Stevens Street homes focused their energies on modifying the construction details. They adapted the building enclosure and the specifications of the HVAC, water heating, lighting, and major appliances to meet the performance standards of Phius and the Zero Ready programs. Computer-based energy modeling tools were central to this process, allowing students to test different options for insulation, window specifications, equipment efficiencies, and other specific construction details.

David Bitter, a Phius Certified Consultant, and Bruce Kitchell, a Phius Certified Rater, volunteered their services on House 66 and provided critical expertise at this stage of the process. Kitchell stayed on the project team for House 68. In Hinson's view, the Stevens Street homes could not have been completed without the help of Bitter, Kitchell, and a host of other technical experts. "We were lucky to have a generous team of creative people supporting the faculty and student teams on the Stevens Street homes," Hinson said. "The give and take between the students and faculty with these experts was one of the most important learning experiences of the project."

The student teams for Houses 66 and 68 also developed new approaches to the exterior cladding design and foundations to adapt the Buster's House prototype to the Opelika sites. Both homes feature an elevated slab foundation system, fiber cement siding, and metal roofs. The Stevens Street homes were also the first homes built for AO Habitat to incorporate the FORTIFIED program standards designed to improve their resilience to damage from high wind conditions.[5] Auburn faculty member Mackenzie Stagg joined the project team midsemester and spearheaded the incorporation of the FORTIFIED details on both projects.

The House 68 team used the experience of building House 66, the associated construction cost history, and a new round of energy modeling to identify key places where they believed construction costs could be reduced without significantly compromising energy performance. These included changes to the insulation strategy at the foundation and in the walls and attic, changes to the window and exterior door systems, and minor changes in the mechanical equipment—primarily related to the active ventilation system.

Construction Process

The design stage on both homes occurred in the initial five weeks of each spring semester (2018 and 2019). As the architecture students pivoted from design to construction planning, they were joined by students from Auburn's construction management program, led by faculty member Mike Hosey. Hosey and his student teams helped plan the construction sequencing and worked alongside the architecture students to construct the homes.

Overall air tightness of the building envelope was a key concern of both the Phius and Zero Ready standards. To ensure that each home was on track to achieve its target, Kitchell performed blower door tests at three stages: after sheathing and window installation, after insulating the walls, and at final completion. The students utilized infrared cameras to identify air leaks during the first two tests, leading to better-than-expected air sealing outcomes on both homes.

The spring semester teams brought each home to the stage where the homes were weather-tight, and a second group of students worked alongside community volunteers and the future homeowners to complete the homes the following summers. The homes were dedicated in September 2018 and 2019, respectively.

After the homeowners moved in, Hinson and Stagg began side-by-side monitoring of energy use in both homes. The monitoring equipment provided circuit-level detail, allowing the team to distinguish between energy use for heating and cooling the home and energy use associated with water heating, large appliances, and lighting. Two years' worth of data collection provides a valuable picture of the balance between energy performance investments at the construction stage and the resulting energy savings. Both homes are very efficient, using less than a third of the energy normally needed to heat and cool a comparable home in this region. As expected, House 66 (Phius certified) uses less energy to heat and cool the home than House 68 (Zero Ready). However, the construction cost savings realized on House 68 more than offset the difference in energy use.[6]

Key Lessons

The Stevens Street homes are an excellent example of a partnership centered on developing new insights that could be folded back into future homes. The collaboration with Auburn University provided AO Habitat with both advanced expertise in building performance and a partner who could absorb much of the risk of exploring new approaches to construction. The record of prior collaborations between Grantham and Hinson provided a foundation of trust that gave both parties confidence that the ambitious goals of the project were achievable. The Stevens Street collaboration has improved the energy efficiency of future Habitat AO projects, even if they are built using standard practices, as well as the pride of the homeowners and community. "These homes are an image of Habitat to the community, to our leaders, to the people that see them," Grantham said. "They see they are beautiful, quality homes, and the homeowners maintain them well."

For Hinson and Hosey, the students' hands-on learning experience was a key project outcome. "The experience of translating what they've studied about building construction and building performance into a completed home adds so much to the students' understanding of these topics," Hosey said. "They come away from these experiences with a much deeper understanding of what it takes to achieve these results."

While beyond-code energy performance upgrades are becoming more commonplace in Habitat for Humanity homes, affiliates rarely have the capacity to do detailed evaluations of the efficacy and impact of these approaches. This makes the perspective gained by the post occupancy performance analysis of the Stevens Street homes all the more important. The faculty research team is working to ensure that the insights reach audiences well beyond the project's direct stakeholders, sharing its work with audiences at the National Habitat for Humanity Affiliate Conference in 2022 and at several national academic and professional conferences within the design disciplines.

Stevens Street homes site plan

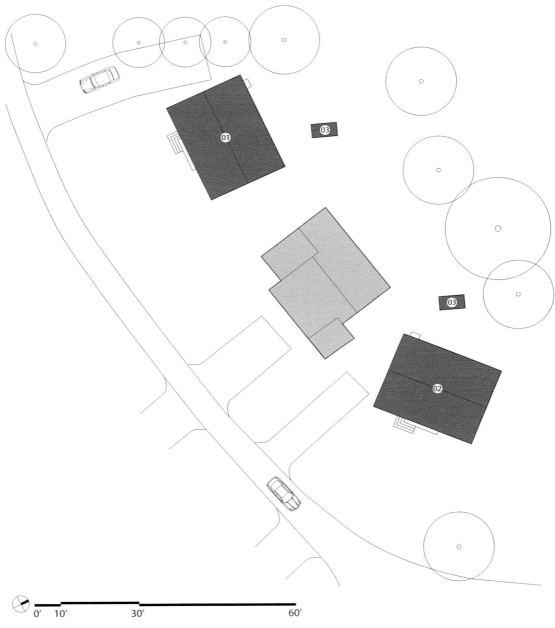

0' 10'   30'   60'

1 House 66
2 House 68
3 Storage Sheds with PV Panels

Stevens Street homes floor plan

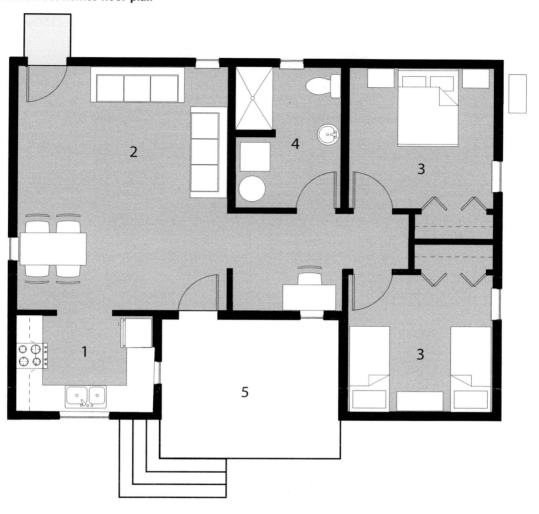

1 Kitchen
2 Living Room
3 Bedroom
4 Bathroom
5 Entry Porch

View of House 66 from the street

View of House 66 from the street

View of the House 66 living area

STEVENS STREET HOMES 43

View of the House 68 kitchen

View of the entry porch at House 68

STEVENS STREET HOMES

View of House 68 from the street

Chapter 4

Empowerhouse

Washington, DC

Habitat for Humanity® of Washington, DC; Parsons School of Design and Milano School of International Affairs, Management, and Urban Policy at The New School; and Stevens Institute of Technology

Key Partnerships

Andrew Modley (Senior Site Supervisor) and Dan Hines (Site Supervisor), Habitat for Humanity of Washington, DC

Laura Briggs (Senior Critic), David Lewis (Professor of Architecture and Dean of Parsons School of Constructed Environments), and Joel Towers (Dean and Professor of Architecture and Sustainable Design), Parsons School of Design, The New School

Program Summary

Single-family attached duplex

3-bedroom, 2-bathroom units

1,350 square feet per unit

2,700 square feet total

Project Overview

Empowerhouse is a two-family duplex built to Passive House standards.[1] The house—developed as a collaboration between The New School's Parsons School of Design and Milano School of International Affairs, and Management, and Urban Policy; Stevens Institute of Technology; and Habitat for Humanity of Washington, DC—was first built on the National Mall in Washington, DC, as an entry in the 2011 US Department of Energy Solar Decathlon. Following the decathlon, the house was relocated to the Greater Deanwood neighborhood of Washington, DC, and expanded into a two-family home for Habitat for Humanity partner families.[2]

DOI: 10.4324/9781003253501-4

Project Process

In 2009, faculty at The New School's Parsons School of Design and the Stevens Institute of Technology were in the early phases of planning for the 2011 US Department of Energy Solar Decathlon.[3] The faculty leading the project envisioned Empowerhouse as a project that would serve as a student educational experience and demonstration home for the competition as well as an advanced innovative design focused on affordability.

The team identified several objectives for the project: performing well in the competition's affordability category, becoming a tool for knowledge transfer, and serving as a model for an affordable Passive House design. Additionally, they wanted the house to remain in Washington, DC, after the competition.

Colleagues from the Milano School of International Affairs reached out to contacts at the Department of Housing and Community Development and were able to connect the team with several nonprofit housing providers in the Washington, DC, area. The faculty team traveled to Washington, DC, in 2009 for a series of meetings to identify a project partner. The team quickly realized that Habitat for Humanity of Washington, DC (Habitat DC) would be an ideal partner, as the affiliate had been steadily advancing its building performance and was ready to build zero-energy homes.

Design Process

With Habitat DC committed as a partner, the faculty from Parsons and the Stevens Institute began designing a set of courses and experiences that, over the span of two years, would engage more than 200 students across multiple degree programs in architecture, design, engineering, communications, management, and urban policy. As the team began the design process, faculty contacted the Passive House Institute to set up a series of training sessions for both students and Habitat DC team members.

The design and engineering problem posed to the students was challenging. The students designed an entry to compete in the ten judged events of the Solar Decathlon. Additionally, the students were to design to

Phius standards and build in flexibility to convert the house for a Habitat DC partner family.

At the outset of the design process, students met with Habitat DC to discuss the approach to constructability, to consider the practicality and replicability of construction undertaken with volunteers, and to identify a project site. Located in the Greater Deanwood neighborhood, the site parcel Habitat DC selected was large enough to accommodate a duplex, and the team was asked to design with this in mind. For the faculty, this provided an opportunity to test the knowledge transfer goal embedded in the collaboration. The faculty and student team would build the first home and modify it once it was relocated to the Deanwood site. Habitat DC would lead the construction of the second half of the duplex.

With a complex set of objectives, the design went through several iterations as different groups of students carried the work forward. Laura Briggs, senior critic at Parsons, credited student presentations and student leadership, as well as shared communication platforms, for the continuity of the project's design intent. Student leaders—some of whom participated in multiple phases of the project—communicated the design direction to the next cohort working on the project. While this work advanced, the faculty established several milestone deadlines. The faculty and student teams worked to secure material and equipment donations according to their deadlines. The affiliate was not asked to contribute any more funding than its typical cost of construction to the project, so the team secured offset funding for the project. Joel Towers, Parsons Professor of Architecture and Sustainable Design, noted that during these deadlines, the faculty determined whether the project would advance.

The design entry for the Solar Decathlon developed into a compact 1,000-square-foot modular structure with one bedroom, one bathroom, and a second-story loft that functioned as a large skylight for the house. The design anticipated the changes that would be necessary once the house was relocated to its final site. To meet Habitat DC's design standards, the house was designed for a 350-square-foot addition consisting

50 EMPOWERHOUSE

of an added second floor that provided an additional bathroom, two bedrooms, and a rooftop terrace with planters for a vegetable garden. The expanded design could house two to four additional people.

Construction Process

In late 2010, student teams from the Stevens Institute and Parsons began construction on Empowerhouse. The initial construction involved the fabrication of two modules in New Jersey. The students were joined by the team from Habitat DC during this phase of construction. Habitat DC's Andrew Modley, Senior Site Supervisor, recalled that seeing the house during initial construction proved valuable once the project was moved to its final site.

In the early spring of 2011, the student team completed the construction of the two modules, which were delivered by truck to the National Mall in Washington, DC, and entered in the Solar Decathlon competition. This entry was the result of over two years of work involving more than 30 faculty members, 200 students from two academic institutions, and key members of Habitat DC—including one of the homeowner families. The collaborative team won the competition's affordability category.

After the close of the competition, Empowerhouse was moved to the Deanwood neighborhood, and the combined team worked together to construct the second floor addition before moving on to the other half of the duplex. Briggs noted that there was only one change from the first house: the students had designed splayed window openings intended to introduce more light into the house. These were simplified in the other half of the duplex Habitat DC built. Hines noted that changes to the window detail did not impact the energy performance of the house and were the only real alteration that the Habitat team made. Hines also credited Modley and Habitat DC for ensuring that the house was built as specified and to Phius standards. The homes were completed and occupied in 2013, and the school continued to work with Habitat DC through the Passive House commissioning process.

Key Lessons

Both the design team and the Habitat affiliate experienced a shift in thinking during the project. They came to understand that the key to affordable construction is the impact of heating and cooling on operational costs. Designing with the homeowners' occupied expenses in mind helped reduce the costs.

David Lewis, architecture professor at The New School, noted, "As an academic institution, the goal was to disseminate information—both what worked and what the challenges [were]." It was critical to share information in a way that "there was an ownership of both the information and the process." Modley noted that the Phius training was valuable experience for the affiliate, as was the team's involvement in the construction phase in New Jersey before the project arrived in DC. The team was able to align their objectives early in the collaboration, and the knowledge gained about Phius has allowed Habitat DC to continue to build Passive House homes. According to Modley, Habitat DC has built six houses to Passive House standards in the years following the Empowerhouse collaboration and continues to build to this standard.

Though the project was an academic organizational challenge, Lewis reflected that its potential to impact "how one builds highly energy-efficient affordable housing—particularly with Habitat—is huge."

Empowerhouse site plan

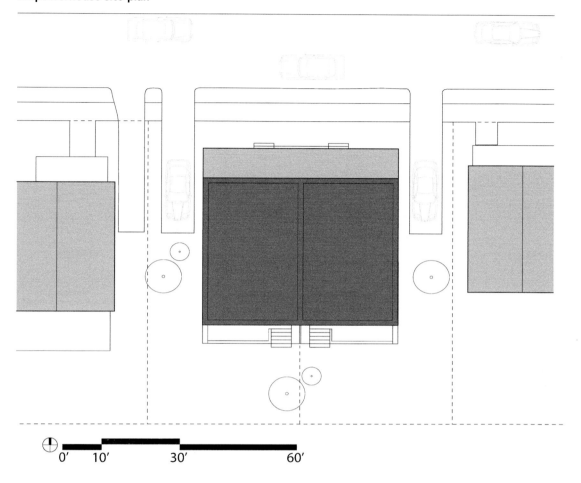

EMPOWERHOUSE 53

Empowerhouse floor plans

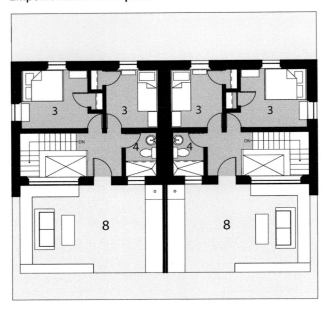

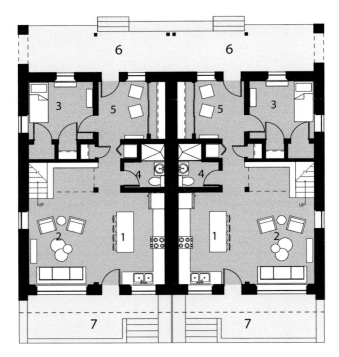

1 Kitchen
2 Living Room
3 Bedroom
4 Bathroom
5 Entry
6 Entry Porch
7 Back Porch
8 Roof Terrace

View of Empowerhouse from the street

View of Empowerhouse porch from the street

View of Empowerhouse from the rear yard

View of Empowerhouse second level roof deck

View to the roof deck and living room from stair

EMPOWERHOUSE

View of the living room

Chapter 5

Seymour Street

Middlebury, Vermont
Habitat for Humanity® of Addison County, Middlebury College, and McLeod Kredell Architects

Key Partnerships

Steve Ingram (President) and Ashley Cadwell (Building Committee Chair), Habitat for Humanity of Addison County

John McLeod (Associate Professor), Middlebury College, and (Principal), McLeod Kredell Architects

Program Summary

Two single-family detached houses

2-bedroom, 1-bath units

1,080 square feet

Featured

3-bedroom, 1-bath unit

1,280 square feet

Project Overview

The two houses on Seymour Street in Middlebury, Vermont, are the result of a collaboration between Habitat for Humanity of Addison County (Habitat Addison County) and Middlebury College's Department of Architecture. The homes were built to exceed Vermont's highest energy standards and advance Habitat of Addison County's construction of energy-efficient housing. Both houses achieved net-zero energy use through the addition of solar panels. Representatives from the college worked with the town of Middlebury and Habitat Addison County to develop the two net-zero houses that sit on a single lot in the downtown area.[1]

DOI: 10.4324/9781003253501-5

Catalysts for Collaboration

Habitat Addison County is a small, all-volunteer affiliate that builds one house per year. In 2017, Habitat Addison County was completing its tenth house—the last in a series of four homes designed to achieve higher levels of energy performance than the affiliate's previous houses. Driven by shifts in the residential energy code and the benefits of improved energy efficiency for homeowners, Habitat Addison County engaged Elizabeth Terwilliger, an architect at Vermont Integrated Architects, to help design this series of four houses and advance its experience with energy-efficient design and construction techniques.

When Addison County Community Trust donated a parcel in downtown Middlebury to Habitat Addison County, the group was in the process of completing construction on the last of the four energy-efficient homes. At the same time, Ashley Cadwell was invited to serve as the chair of the Habitat Addison County Building Committee, and contractor Alex Carver joined the Board of Directors. These additions would turn out to be critical to the collaboration between Middlebury College and the affiliate.

Cadwell approached John McLeod, principal of McLeod Kredell Architects and Middlebury professor, about collaborating on a house design for Habitat Addison County's 11th site. Together with Middlebury Department Chair Peter Broucke, the pair developed a curriculum in which architecture students would design the house and investigate specific topics: energy efficiency and context.

The design process would need to align with both the academic calendar and Habitat Addison County's construction calendar, which was typically one house per year with construction beginning in the spring. The program structured the collaboration over three academic terms. The spring studio would initiate the project, the fall course would advance the technical drawings for pricing and permitting, and the four-week January term would finalize the construction drawings for permit and pricing.

Design Process

With agreements and a curriculum model in place for the collaboration, the Seymour Street project began in the spring of 2018 as a pilot design studio. McLeod tasked the students with the design of two energy-efficient homes sited on a single lot in downtown Middlebury. The spring semester began with site and precedent research and analysis. As students studied the site and zoning, they discovered they could fit two houses on the site and meet all of the required zoning setbacks, and they proceeded to develop design options for the houses. McLeod's goal for the studio was to have a single design in place at the end of the term. To facilitate the process, students worked in teams to develop a range of possible designs for the site.

As McLeod recalled, Cadwell and Steve Ingram, the Habitat Addison County president, participated in the studio weekly to narrow options until the design for the two houses was well established. Once the design was settled, the students presented the proposal multiple times to the town's Development Review Board. As McLeod recalled, the team encountered some challenges during this phase of the semester, the first of which concerned the placement of buildings on the site.

The downtown site was not an official historic district but locally had been considered as such. Seymour Street was lined with houses and buildings that were set back similarly from the sidewalk and all had gable ends facing the street. The students' initial proposals looked at different ways to situate the projects on the site and pulled back from the established setback. Meanwhile, Middlebury's Development Review Board preferred that the front house maintain a similar setback to adjacent structures. To address the context, the student team adopted a contemporary take on the vernacular structures of the area and developed a simple gable form that reflected the surrounding architecture while providing a progressive image for affordable housing.

After revising the site layout and aligning with the existing buildings on the street, the team ran into another obstacle. As described, there were both substantive and perceived concerns voiced in the Development Review Board meetings—the most significant of which regarded lot size. During the review process, the town notified the team that the lot size was actually not large enough to accommodate two dwellings, being around 3,000 square feet too small. After some title research, Habitat Addison County contacted the owner of a large parcel behind the Seymour Street site and requested to purchase the land necessary to meet the town's area requirement. The property owner eventually donated the land to Habitat Addison County, allowing the project to move forward as a two-house development.

In addition to these challenges, the project faced discouraging questions on whether or not it was a good idea to put affordable housing in downtown Middlebury. Cadwell was impressed with the students' professionalism during public forums and their navigation through the approval process.

The town approved the project at the end of the fall term, and the next two terms were dedicated to developing final drawings for the project. The fall semester cohort developed the drawings for a 75% construction document set. During the January term, a smaller team of students completed the drawings and delivered the set to Habitat Addison County for permitting.

Construction Process

The program was structured to focus on the design and documentation process; however, students were able to volunteer on the construction project during a build day the following fall semester. The construction of the house posed some challenges for Habitat Addison County, but the appointment of Alex Carver to the Board of Directors provided additional expertise for the group's construction experience. Carver's background as a local contractor allowed the team to move forward with confidence on some of the design's more refined details. Through a state grant program,[2] Habitat Addison County was able install solar panels on the house, which allowed the homes to achieve nearly net-zero energy use.

The construction of the first house was completed in December 2018, and the second house was completed the following year. During that time, McLeod started another group of students on a new collaboration to design a four-house development in the Booth Woods neighborhood in nearby Vergennes, Vermont.

Key Lessons

The Seymour Street houses marked the start of an ongoing collaboration among Middlebury College, McLeod Kredell Architects, and Habitat Addison County. In addition to tracking net-zero energy use, the houses have received multiple design awards, including a 2020 AIA Vermont Honor Award. McLeod credited Cadwell for imagining the collaboration, and they both credited the weekly meetings during the design phase for aligning expectations and maintaining focus on the collaborative goals.

Ingram noted that the affiliate's work with the local architect before the Middlebury partnership gave the organization expertise in increasing energy-efficiency requirements. With this experience and Alex Carver's additional layer of construction experience, the affiliate was more comfortable taking on the design challenges that the students proposed.

Ingram also described a shift in focus as a result of the work on the Seymour Street homes. Over the course of this project, the affiliate shifted to focus on the site location and the impact that proximity to schools, grocery stores, and work have on a family's monthly budget in order to directly benefit the homeowners' lives. Cadwell echoed this sentiment, noting that the next project the affiliate would begin, Booth Woods, was ideal because it was located within walking distance of the downtown area of Vergennes, Vermont.

From McLeod's perspective, the experience allowed the college and the students to engage directly and build relationships within the community. As McLeod noted, the collaboration has been a success and continues to be refined, folding in new experiences for student involvement in the projects.

Seymour Street site plan

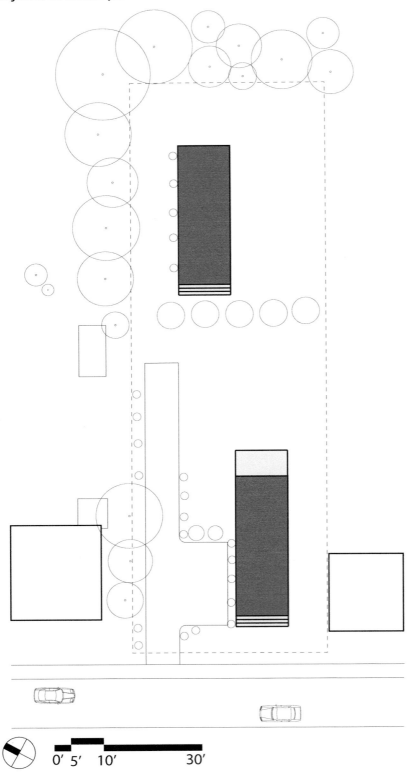

Seymour Street floor plan

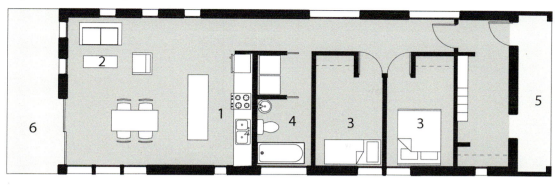

0' 1' 5'   10'   20'

1 Kitchen
2 Living Room
3 Bedroom
4 Bathroom
5 Entry Porch
6 Rear Porch

View of the entry porch

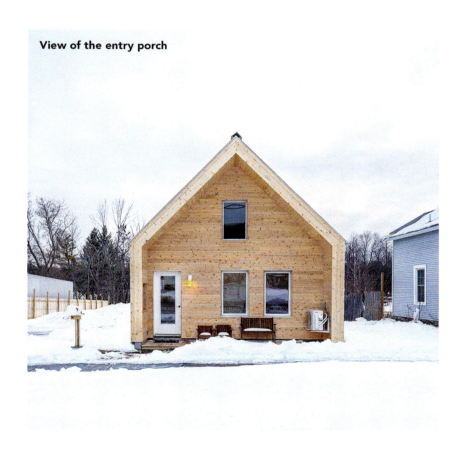

SEYMOUR STREET   67

View from Seymour Street

View of kitchen and dining area

View of the hall to the dining area

View of the living room

View from the rear

Chapter 6

Booth Woods

Vergennes, Vermont

Habitat for Humanity® of Addison County, Middlebury College, and McLeod Kredell Architects

Key Partnerships

Steve Ingram (President) and Ashley Cadwell (Building Committee Chair), Habitat for Humanity of Addison County

John McLeod (Associate Professor), Middlebury College and (Principal), McLeod Kredell Architects

Program Summary

Four single-family detached houses

Featured

One 4-bedroom, 2-bath unit

1,400 square feet

One 2/3-bedroom, 2-bath flex unit

1,200 square feet

Two 2/3-bedroom, 1-bath flex unit

1,200 square feet

Project Overview

The four-house development in the Booth Woods neighborhood of Vergennes, Vermont, is the result of the collaboration between Habitat for Humanity of Addison County (Habitat Addison County) and Middlebury College's Department of Architecture that began in 2018 with the design and construction of the Seymour Street houses in Middlebury, Vermont.[1] The project was initiated as a master planning study, testing the ability to develop a topographically challenging site within walking distance of downtown Vergennes. A set of four homes was designed to exceed Vermont's highest energy standards and advance Habitat Addison County's construction of energy-efficient housing and flexible design.[2]

DOI: 10.4324/9781003253501-6

Catalysts for Collaboration

As construction concluded on the first Seymour Street house, Habitat Addison County received a large parcel of land in Vergennes, Vermont. The new parcel presented an opportunity to continue the collaboration between the affiliate and Middlebury College.

Steve Ingram, Habitat Addison County President, and Ashley Cadwell, Habitat Addison County Building Committee Chair, discussed the site and collaboration opportunity with John McLeod, principal of McLeod Kredell Architects and Middlebury professor, in 2018. Together, they decided to study the site in a spring semester studio. The site was within walking distance of the downtown area of Vergennes; however, as Ingram noted, it had remained undeveloped due to the site's challenging topography. McLeod focused the spring studio on an analysis of what could be built.

Design Process

In the spring of 2019, McLeod worked with the students to develop designs for an in-town neighborhood of four houses in Vergennes. In contrast to Middlebury, the zoning requirements and municipal regulations were less restrictive, and the primary challenge of the site was the topography. The steep slope and narrow site limited the development options. The students worked through a series of site designs for a micro-neighborhood that accommodated a set of houses and shared spaces. The initial site schemes proposed both a solar and community garden in addition to the homes. The students developed four individual parcels organized along the same side of the road, each with a corresponding storage shed that established the boundary of the drive and provided a unique element for each house. The houses were situated such that the properties were all on one side of the road. The sites sloped up steeply behind the houses to a wooded ridge that was used as a walking trail by the neighborhood. The land across the road from the houses was wooded and undeveloped and was intended to remain that way. While the community garden and solar gardens were not realized, the woodland buffer provided a shared landscape for the micro-neighborhood.

The students developed the site plan and constructed a physical site model for the proposed development. The model was displayed in the Vergennes city planning office. As Ingram recalled, the city planner and town were fully persuaded by the students' models and drawings of the Booth Woods homes.

Following the site design phase, the studio focused on the house plans. From the outset, the team had identified a goal of building net-zero energy homes. Cadwell recalled that both McLeod and Habitat Addison County wanted to introduce other considerations. Among the collaboration objectives was a goal to develop a set of designs that would accommodate homeowner needs without knowing who the homeowners would be—essentially, flexibility within the design.

The first house designed for the site was a two-story, three- to four-bedroom flex house. The house could accommodate a larger family or provide a flex space within the home to be used as a home office or study space for the prospective family. While it was designed first, the two-story house was not the first home built in the neighborhood.

As the team completed the design of the first house in Booth Woods, Habitat Addison County was nearing completion of the second house on Seymour Street in Middlebury. At this time, Cadwell was interested in moving forward with the design of the second and third houses in Booth Woods. This would allow the affiliate to have a set of plans ready as the family selection committee worked to match a family to a home. Ingram and Cadwell wanted the next two homes to be accessible and incorporate the spatial adaptability of the flex room.

McLeod and the students began the design of the two houses in the spring of 2020. The studio continued to meet with Habitat Addison County as they worked to meet Americans with Disabilities Act (ADA) guidelines. The houses were designed as two-bedroom flex homes with a third room that could be used as a bedroom, as a home office, or for other use as the family's needs determined.

As the design progressed, the size of the ADA bathroom proved to be a challenge in the small house. McLeod recalled members of the affiliate noting that the bathroom was really big. In a small house, the impact was substantial, and the team sought ways to increase the utility of the space while meeting ADA guidelines.

Construction Process

During the summer of 2020, McLeod led a design-build workshop in Vergennes to construct the first Booth Woods storage shed. A recurring summer event by McLeod Kredell Architects, the workshop included students from Middlebury as well as academic institutions from across the country.[3] During the workshop in the following summer (2021), the second storage shed was completed for the micro-neighborhood.

The sheds were sited in the front of each house, helping to establish the entry to the homes and giving each home a unique element along the street. Cadwell noted that the sheds were a great addition and that their construction prior to that of the house gave the building crew a place to store equipment and materials onsite during the home construction.

The second house designed was the first built. McLeod noted that the family did not have any specific need for the accessible features; however, the integrated accessibility of the design ensured that the home was future-ready. Habitat Addison County's continued involvement with the neighborhood will ensure that the housing remains affordable and accessible.

As construction started on the third house, McLeod and Habitat Addison County turned their attention to the design of the fourth house in Booth Woods. Ingram recalled, "We wanted to issue the students a challenge on every home. We want to build highly energy-efficient and very green homes. On this last home, we challenged them to find a way not to use concrete." McLeod and the students were excited to take on the challenge of a concrete-free house for the final collaboration. The house was also designed as a net-zero, two- to three-bedroom flex plan.

Key Lessons

While not yet complete, the Booth Woods collaboration provided Habitat Addison County an opportunity to work with Middlebury faculty and students to explore new improvements for affordable housing. Ingram was quick to note that the students' professionalism was key to the success of the collaboration. Ingram and Cadwell said that their presentation of the design work—plans, renderings, and physical models—in public presentations helped the projects move forward.

Not only were individuals in the public impressed, the students' work was instrumental in assuring Habitat Addison County's Board of Directors that the projects were achievable. "The board had never seen perspectives, renderings, models like this," Ingram said. "They have been flabbergasted by the breadth and professionalism of the student presentations."

Booth Woods site plan

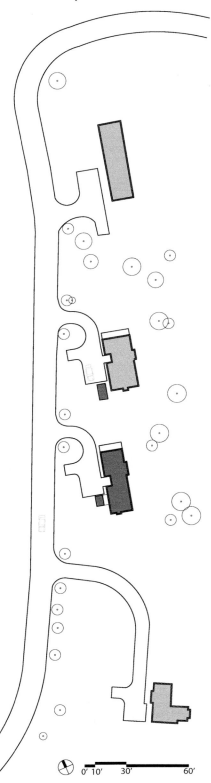

Booth Woods floor plan

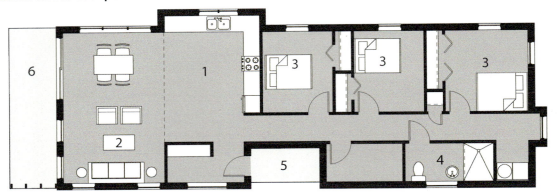

1. Kitchen
2. Living Room
3. Bedroom
4. Bathroom
5. Entry Porch
6. Porch

Aerial view of House 14 (House 16 under construction beyond)

View from the road

View of the house and patio

BOOTH WOODS

View from the rear

View of the house and storage building

Aerial view of House 14 with photovoltaic panels on roof

Chapter 7

Grand Avenue Duplexes and Basalt Vista

Silt, Colorado
Habitat for Humanity® of the Roaring Fork Valley and 2757 design co.

Basalt Vista

Basalt, Colorado
Habitat for Humanity of the Roaring Fork Valley and 2757 design co.

Key Partnerships

Jake Ezratty (Construction Manager–Basalt Vista), Habitat for Humanity of the Roaring Fork Valley
Erica Stahl Golden, AIA (Principal), 2757 design co.

Grand Avenue Duplexes Program Summary

Four-unit duplex development
3-bedroom, 2-bath, and den units
1,530 square feet per unit
Each with 1-car garage

Basalt Vista Program Summary

27-unit duplex and triplex development

Two 2-bedroom, 1.5-bath units

1,120 square feet

Two 2-bedroom, 2-bath units

1,230 square feet

Seventeen 3-bedroom, 2-bath units

1,500 square feet

Six 4-bedroom, 2-bath units

1,650 square feet

Each with garages or covered parking and integrated exterior storage

Project Overview

Basalt Vista, a 27-unit net-zero development, is the result of a collaboration involving the Habitat for Humanity of the Roaring Fork Valley (Habitat RFV), 2757 design co. (2757), the Roaring Fork Valley School District, Pitkin County, Aspen Community Office of Resource Efficiency (Aspen CORE), Holy Cross Electric Association (HCE), and National Renewable Energy Laboratories (NREL). The project, designed and built over a six-year period, was adapted multiple times to respond to many external factors that the team encountered, including local wildfires, the COVID-19 pandemic, and extreme cost escalation. During the approvals timeline of the Basalt Vista project, Habitat RFV and 2757 design co. also designed and developed the Grand Avenue Duplexes, a pair of duplexes in Silt, Colorado, that served as a pilot project for Basalt Vista.[1]

Catalysts for Collaboration

In 2015, Erica Golden and Brian Golden, principals at 2757, founded their architecture firm in Carbondale, Colorado. The pair was interested in establishing a practice with a focus on affordable housing. Previously, both Erica and Brian worked at CCY Architects in Basalt, Colorado, where they first met with Habitat RFV during a master planning design charrette for Basalt Vista.

Erica Golden recalled that Scott Gilbert, then-president of Habitat RFV, was looking for unique, out-of-the-box ways to provide more affordable workforce housing. Increasing land and construction costs led to a master planning exercise focused on finding ways to unlock unused land to develop workforce housing. Working with the Roaring Fork Valley School District and Pitkin County, the team developed a master plan for a 27-unit neighborhood on land owned by the school district behind the Basalt High School. The school district donated approximately eight acres of the site, and Pitkin County committed approximately $3 million in infrastructure and site development costs. Habitat RFV agreed to set aside half of the units for school district employees and the other half for the Aspen Pitkin County Housing Authority.

The master plan advanced through a year-and-a-half–long approvals process, during which time Habitat RFV was able to complete a multiunit development in Silt, Colorado. The affiliate had acquired the land below market value during the previous recession and was waiting for a gap in its schedule to develop.

Habitat RFV asked 2757 to develop the design for a three-duplex development on Grand Avenue in Silt, Colorado. Erica Golden said the project was a great opportunity to continue to work with Habitat RFV and learn more about the affiliate's construction process.

Grand Avenue Duplexes

The Grand Avenue site was a set of narrow lots that needed only minor lot line adjustments. The approvals process was much quicker for

Grand Avenue, and the team began developing the designs for the site. Golden noted that the width of the sites dictated the layout of the duplexes. The narrowness of the lots led to a dense linear configuration of the three duplex units.[2] Rather than sharing a long party wall, the units shared a short end wall. The site configuration created units that had good exposure to daylight as well as drive access and parking between units.

The porches became a focus of the design. Each unit has a deep porch that organized the main entry to the house and provided a semi-enclosed outdoor living space. Throughout the design of the Grand Avenue duplexes, the team gained valuable experience in understanding and working with Habitat RFV's construction methods. As Golden noted, the design team had not had much experience working with precut studs and prefabricated assemblies, and they used the experience on the Grand Avenue duplexes to learn how to design to Habitat RFV's standards.

For the Grand Avenue duplexes, the design team found the opportunity to enhance the projects through focused attention and material detail at the porches. Each home has a unique material pattern and color at the porch, adding an individuating element to each home. The homes on Grand Avenue were completed in 2018 as the work on Basalt Vista was about to resume.

Basalt Vista

Once approval for the Basalt Vista development was secured, site development began. The site was an undeveloped area of land behind the high school and required all new site infrastructure. As the site was prepared, the team planned a three-phase construction process. Each phase would include nine of the 27 units, and, per the approvals, the playground site amenity was able to be completed by the second phase.

Many of the lessons learned on the Grand Avenue duplexes were incorporated over the course of the project. Golden noted that the houses were designed for prefabrication and to incorporate the typical anticipated material donations Habitat RFV received through national partnerships as well as local in-kind donations.

Golden described the design of the homes as rather straightforward. The homes were designed to be highly energy efficient through robust air sealing, high levels of insulation, and carefully designed conditioning systems. The duplexes and triplexes have a simple floor plan and interior volume with careful attention to natural light. Openings were organized to maximize daylight and capture views of the valley below. The team at 2757 sought to emphasize the porches and entry of each home with exposed framing, adding additional detail to these areas of the homes and encouraging the homeowners to spend time outside, creating community vitality along the street.

The designs stayed generally the same throughout the three phases of construction; however, the construction systems varied phase to phase due to changing circumstances around the project, including a local wildfire, a pandemic and subsequent extreme material cost escalation, and difficulty sourcing materials.

Construction on phase one began in 2018. Jake Ezratty, construction manager for Habitat RFV, recalled that gas service was about to be extended to the site when the team was presented with a set of partnerships that would allow the development to pursue net-zero energy for each residence. The houses had been designed to be highly energy efficient, and, as Erica Golden noted, and it was relatively simple to make minor adjustments in order to accommodate air source heat pumps and heat pump water heaters. The increased cost of those systems was offset by a grant offered by Aspen CORE.[3] When the team decided to pursue net-zero goals, Aspen CORE worked as an energy consultant and utilized funding through the Pitkin County Renewable Energy Mitigation Program to also provide photovoltaic (PV) arrays for each residence.[4]

Holy Cross Energy (HCE), the electrical service provider for the site, partnered with the National Renewable Energy Laboratory (NREL) to participate in a grid resilience pilot study with the first four houses and to assist in achieving net-zero energy use.[5] The four houses in the pilot study incorporated a battery tied to the PV array and the utility's electric service grid. NREL and HCE monitored the home's energy use—each individually metered—and the ability for the utility to draw energy from the batteries back into the utility's electrical service grid. Other than the battery, the following homes in the neighborhood were built to the same energy efficiency standards and with the same high-efficiency mechanical and electrical systems as the pilot homes.

The homes in phase one were built with prefabricated wall panels and roof trusses and made use of partnerships that Habitat for Humanity International had established for affiliates around the country.[6] Ezratty said, "The team at 2757 did a great job of working with the materials and donations Habitat RFV received. They advocated for assemblies that incorporated DOW blue board (rigid insulation) because at the time we were getting the material donated."

Just before the team began phase two, Habitat RFV transitioned leadership, and Gail Schwartz began her term as president. Schwartz's start coincided with the end of the partnership that provided rigid blue board insulation. This led the team to shift assembly strategies while still maintaining the energy performance goals of the project. The team decided to utilize structurally insulated panels (SIPs) for the houses in phase two. The houses were each built on separate parcels and were permitted individually during each phase of construction, giving the team the ability to adjust and tune the design as changes in materials and systems occurred. Ezratty noted that the SIP system worked well to meet the air sealing and insulation requirements for the net-zero homes, but the installation of the electrical components was slower due to the novelty of the system for Habitat RFV.

As phase two neared completion, construction was interrupted by the COVID-19 pandemic, and progress slowed. Construction halted for several months during the height of the pandemic. Once the county allowed construction sites to resume, the project not only faced a smaller volunteer pool but also supply chain delays and price fluctuations. The SIPs suddenly became too expensive for the project as wood product prices soared.[7] The team decided to switch to ZIP System® panels for the houses in phase three. In addition to the material cost and lead time fluctuations the team was encountering, Pitkin County had adopted a new fire regulation, Firewise, that required a revision of the exterior finishes and exposed framing of the porches for the last phase of the project.

The team wanted to ensure that the neighborhood was cohesive and worked to resolve the challenges through a focused evaluation of the house designs. Ezratty and the team removed windows in rooms with more than two windows and changed out material selections where possible to save money but maintain durability.

Golden recalled that during this final phase, the team realized that the homes were still not affordable to some of the school district employees for whom they were designed. The smallest floor plan in phase three was a three-bedroom unit. Golden and the team at 2757 were able to revise units to incorporate additional two-bedroom units without adjusting the foundation that was already under construction.

The exterior materials also changed to more fire-resistant materials during this phase. The biggest change was the porch framing, which was designed with exposed wood members to add more texture at the entries and outdoor living rooms on the downhill side of the houses. The new code required the members to either be encased or be sized larger to classify as heavy timber construction. Habitat RFV decided to continue with the exposed framing to maintain the consistency of the homes in Basalt Vista. The team worked through the changes and completed the project in 2021.

All 27 homes are equipped with a 10-kW PV array, bringing energy use to net zero for the neighborhood. Golden recalled that the homeowners' annual electricity bills averaged out to the cost of the utility company's connection fee—in the summer months in Colorado, a higher amount of energy is generated. Ezratty noted that Habitat RFV created a homeowners association (HOA) for Basalt Vista to cover everything on the outside of the house, including establishing an account for PV repair and replacement. Habitat RFV is currently working on another net-zero development, building on the lessons learned from Basalt Vista.

Key Lessons

Basalt Vista and the Grand Avenue Duplexes are excellent examples of projects in which goal alignment allowed the team to navigate changing circumstances that could have derailed the project. The communication among team members was important, but focus on the broader goals of the project was more critical. The 2757 team was primed to recognize the challenges Habitat for Humanity affiliates face in balancing project goals, homeowner needs, material availability, and construction techniques adapted to skilled and unskilled constructors through the Grand Avenue duplexes.

The phasing of the construction allowed Habitat RFV and 2757 to develop considerable knowledge of multiple construction techniques for designing and constructing net-zero energy use homes. Ezratty noted that the team identified opportunities to improve.

Ezratty explained that the HOA was valuable but that costs for homeowners could be further cut if the PV arrays were not onsite. He said that the affiliate's next project would utilize a solar farm offsite. The displacement of the PV array from the homes would lower the cost of the HOA dues, as the maintenance and replacement of the array would be part of the electrical service agreement. The next project will also be serviced by a different utility company. The more critical lesson may lie in the increasing importance of understanding the energy service environment of project sites.

Basalt Vista also provides an excellent example of leadership. Habitat RFV's leadership team invited key stakeholders—including design professionals—into the project before it was fully defined. The affiliate was willing to engage in unique partnerships to expand the supply of affordable workforce housing and was willing to adapt and shift to even more aggressive goals to accomplish the larger project.

Grand Avenue Duplexes site plan

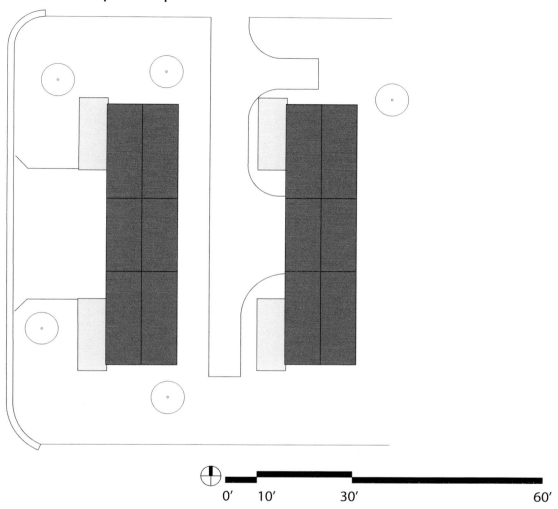

GRAND AVENUE DUPLEXES AND BASALT VISTA

Grand Avenue Duplexes floor plans

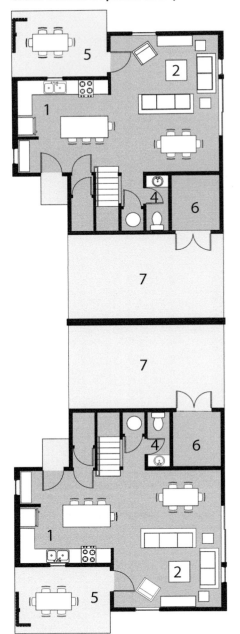
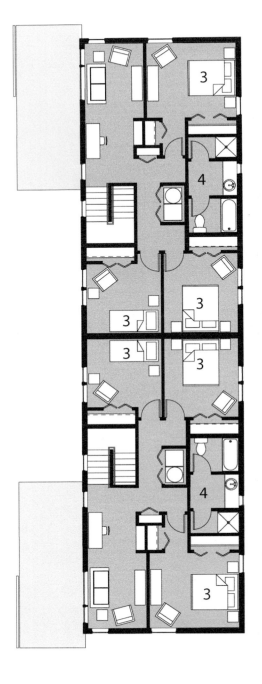

1 Kitchen
2 Living Room
3 Bedroom
4 Bathroom
5 Entry Porch
6 Storage
7 Carport

View from Grand Avenue

View of the entry porch from Grand Avenue

Basalt Vista site plan

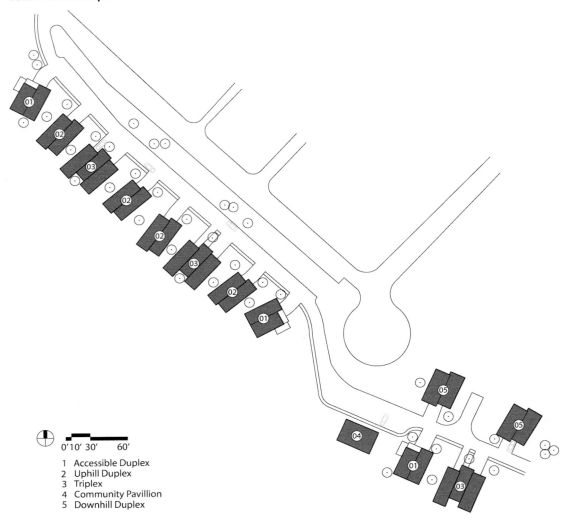

0' 10' 30' 60'

1 Accessible Duplex
2 Uphill Duplex
3 Triplex
4 Community Pavillion
5 Downhill Duplex

Basalt Vista floor plans

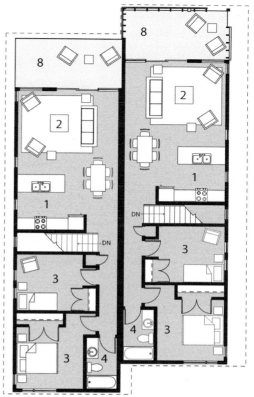

1 Kitchen
2 Living Room
3 Bedroom
4 Bathroom
5 Storage
6 Entry Porch
7 Carport
8 Porch

View of the entry porch

View of the side entry from the car court

Aerial view of Basalt Vista

View of a downhill duplex unit shared entry porch

Aerial view of an uphill duplex unit

View of a triplex unit

View of a downhill duplex unit with the high school in the background

GRAND AVENUE DUPLEXES AND BASALT VISTA

Chapter 8

Habitat Quintana

San Juan, Puerto Rico
Habitat for Humanity® Puerto Rico and Álvarez-Díaz & Villalōn, Architecture & Interior Design

Key Partnerships
Amanda Silva (Executive Director), Habitat for Humanity Puerto Rico
Ricardo Álvarez-Díaz (Principal), Álvarez-Díaz & Villalōn, Architecture & Interior Design

Project Summary
Urban neighborhood context
3-bedroom, 1.5-bath single-family townhomes
1,384 square feet
1-bedroom, 1-bath accessible unit
530 square feet

Project Overview
The Habitat Quintana project is the product of a collaboration between Habitat for Humanity Puerto Rico and Álvarez-Díaz & Villalōn Architecture & Interior Design (AD&V). The three-unit development, located in the Quintana neighborhood of San Juan, was the first new residential project completed on the island of Puerto Rico in the wake of Hurricane Maria.[1]

DOI: 10.4324/9781003253501-8

Catalysts for Collaboration

As Amanda Silva, Executive Director of Habitat for Humanity of Puerto Rico (Habitat Puerto Rico), met with a local bank to sign agreements transferring a parcel of land in the Quintana neighborhood of San Juan, all eyes were on the weather forecast. Two days later, on September 20, 2017, Hurricane Maria devastated the island, leaving thousands of families without homes, power, or clean water.[2]

Established in 1997, Habitat Puerto Rico's primary focus was on repairing and renovating existing homes—the majority of which were built by the homeowners outside of the formal permitting process. At the time of the disaster, the affiliate had one full-time staff member (Silva) and one part-time staff member. According to Ricardo Álvarez-Díaz, principal at AD&V, who had served as a volunteer member of the affiliate's Board of Directors, Habitat Puerto Rico had begun to prioritize building new homes on sites closer to urban centers prior to the hurricane. "We were looking for sites that would help revitalize the urban core [of San Juan], bring people back to the town center, and provide opportunities to develop multifamily homes," Álvarez-Díaz said.

In the aftermath of Hurricane Maria, it was nearly impossible to access most of the island. While most businesses were completely shut down without power for almost a year, AD&V's office was able to stay open by running electrical systems on generators until power was restored in December 2017, nearly three months after the hurricane. The firm never stopped working, although the office, equipped with air conditioning and kitchen facilities, became a shelter for the families of AD&V staff.

While Habitat Puerto Rico assessed where it could best restart its construction activities, Silva reached out to Álvarez-Díaz to solicit AD&V's assistance with the evaluation of site options in the affiliate's portfolio. "When Amanda called, we knew [helping Habitat Puerto Rico] wasn't a choice. It was a responsibility." Álvarez-Díaz said.

Most of the sites available to the affiliate could only accommodate a single home. However, the Quintana site offered the opportunity to construct three homes in a townhome configuration—a typology common to San Juan but new for Habitat Puerto Rico. AD&V agreed to take on the Quintana project for a "low-bono fee"[3] and began design studies in the fall of 2017.

Design Process

By December 2017, AD&V and Habitat Puerto Rico had settled on a scheme that included two two-story, three-bedroom townhomes and a third single-story, one-bedroom unit designed for accessibility on the pie-shaped 6,148-square-foot site. The one-story accessible unit faced the cul-de-sac with the two-story units located behind it on the wider portion of the parcel.

The design of the two-story units placed the bedrooms on the upper level and provided large operable windows to maximize cross ventilation—a design response tailored to Puerto Rico's tropical climate. These units also featured a roof terrace located above the carport that gave each family an outdoor social space above the street level.

The units were designed to comply with the local energy codes and incorporate wall insulation—an uncommon practice in most Puerto Rican homes—to help conserve energy when active cooling systems were in use. Each unit also had photovoltaic panels located on the roof to offset power drawn from the power grid and provide the units with a backup system should service be interrupted.

The units were largely constructed of cast-in-place concrete and concrete block covered with stucco—building systems common in Puerto Rico and appreciated by the public. "We are prone to earthquakes and hurricanes, so we have a mentality of associating concrete construction with safety," Silva said.

Construction Process

With most government offices closed and all resources focused on recovery activities, it took much longer than normal to complete the permitting process. In the spring of 2018, the Quintana project was awarded the first permit for new construction on the island after the hurricane, an accomplishment that helped draw support for Habitat Puerto Rico and attention to the Quintana project.

The concrete and masonry systems incorporated in the design dictated that much of the construction be done by professional contractors. Given the scope of devastation across the island, a volunteer-focused approach to construction would have been impractical. However, with so much of the island's construction sector focused on recovery efforts, securing professional builders for the project was challenging.

The project received a big boost when the US National Guard reached out to offer its help. The National Guard was seeking opportunities to train its units in construction skills associated with disaster recovery and contacted Silva regarding the Quintana project. Soldiers from the New York Army National Guard's 204th Engineer Battalion worked alongside the contractors through the summer of 2018, helping to prepare the site; build concrete formwork; and complete the concrete walls, floors, and roofs.[4]

Contractors, local volunteers, and the selected homeowner families saw the project to completion in early 2019, just six months after the start of construction. As with the original permit reviews, final inspections and occupancy permits took longer than normal to complete, but the homes were dedicated and turned over to the homeowner families in the summer of 2019.

Key Lessons

From Silva's perspective, working with professional architects is paramount to Habitat Puerto Rico's goals. "Design is key," she stated. "Habitat Puerto Rico's main goal is helping our homeowner families achieve a higher quality of life, and we need professionals [like AD&V] to help us make sure everything comes together."

From Álvarez-Díaz's perspective, completing the Habitat Quintana project was a capacity-building experience for Habitat Puerto Rico.

Currently, the affiliate is working closely with Habitat for Humanity International on a hurricane recovery program that includes both renovation and new construction activities, and it has grown to include 20 people on staff.

The Habitat Quintana project is an amazing example of resilience in the face of adversity. According to Álvarez-Díaz, Silva and Habitat Puerto Rico pushed the project through in the face of countless obstacles related to the impact of Hurricane Maria. In his view, the success of the collaboration was closely tied to the stakeholders' common focus: serving the needs of the homeowner families.

For Silva, the commitment of the architects and the contractors proved pivotal to realizing the project in such trying circumstances. "We were blessed with having the right people at the right time."

Habitat Quintana site plan

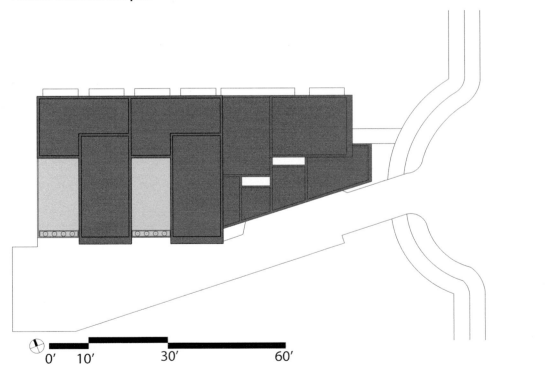

Habitat Quintana floor plans

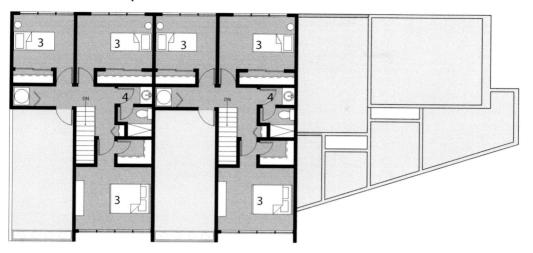

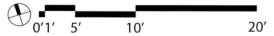

1. Kitchen
2. Living Room
3. Bedroom
4. Bathroom
5. Garage

View of the accessible unit from the street

View of the townhome units

HABITAT QUINTANA   111

View of the entrance at the accessible unit

Ground level interior view of the townhome unit

View of the kitchen at the accessible unit

View of the upper level at the townhome units prior to glazing installation

Chapter 9

Lomita Avenue Townhomes

Glendale, California
San Gabriel Valley Habitat for Humanity® and [au]workshop architects+urbanists

Key Partnerships
Sonja Yates (Executive Director), San Gabriel Valley Habitat for Humanity
Randy Shortridge (Principal), [au]workshop architects+urbanists

Project Summary
Suburban neighborhood context
Six 3-bedroom, 2.5-bath, single-family townhomes
1,285 square feet (two levels) with 395-square-foot attached garage

Project Overview
The Lomita Avenue Townhomes are the product of a collaboration between San Gabriel Valley Habitat for Humanity (SGV Habitat) and [au]workshop architects+urbanists. The six-unit project was developed on the site of two former single-family lots in the heart of Glendale, California, in a rapidly densifying neighborhood of apartment complexes and single-family homes. The project uses compositional patterns of off-center windows and flat roofs with a material palette of fiber cement lap and board-and-batten siding to evoke the aesthetic language of California Modernism.[1]

DOI: 10.4324/9781003253501-9

Design Process

SGV Habitat had cultivated a track record of successful collaborations in many of the 31 communities in and around the San Gabriel Valley area of Los Angeles County, including eight projects with the City of Glendale. When the City of Glendale Housing Authority contacted Sonja Yates, Executive Director of SGV Habitat, in mid-2015 about two adjacent single-family parcels on Lomita Avenue, she turned to Randy Shortridge, principal at [au]workshop architects+urbanists of Fort Collins, Colorado. Shortridge had recently completed a successful partnership with SGV Habitat on a project in nearby Pasadena and had relocated his practice from California to Colorado during the Pasadena project. Nevertheless, Yates was confident Shortridge was the right architect for the Lomita Avenue site. "Randy is a marvelous architect to work with. He always grasps the concept we're working on and responds accordingly," Yates said.

The surrounding neighborhood—once exclusively single-family homes—was rapidly transforming into higher-density housing developments. The priority for SGV Habitat and the Glendale Housing Authority was maximizing the number of affordable homes that could be built on the Lomita Avenue site. Shortridge determined that the site could accommodate six townhomes, four facing the street and two at the rear of the parcel, provided the required parking (two spaces per unit) was incorporated into garages within the ground level of the townhomes.

The townhouse layouts clustered the living, dining, and kitchen spaces on the lower level, along with a half bath. The upper level plan included three bedrooms, two full baths, and a laundry room. A double-height space over the entry and kitchen provided a spatial connection between the two levels. The units at the rear of the property featured the same plan, rotated to allow for entrance on the long side of the ground floor. At 1,285 square feet, the units were slightly larger than SGV Habitat's norm, a result largely attributable to the internal stairs and the additional required half-bath associated with the two-level configuration as well as the need to accommodate parking within the footprint of the lower level.

In contrast to the Pasadena project, which conformed to the city's Craftsman style design standards, the context of the Lomita Avenue site was a more eclectic mix of styles. Nevertheless, the design needed to be compatible with the surrounding market-rate neighborhood. "The key to getting the opportunity [to build on this site] was to have the new Habitat construction fit into the community in a way that it would not cause a big uproar," Yates said.

Shortridge provided SGV Habitat with aesthetic studies of the exteriors that included several style options. They ultimately settled on what he describes as a "California Modern" approach, featuring a palette of lap and board-and-batten fiber cement siding with a bold yellow, dark gray, and white paint scheme. The low-slope roof configuration was chosen, in part, to facilitate future rooftop solar panel installation.

Construction Process

In a process that took over a year to complete, negotiating project approvals with the planning and engineering departments of the City of Glendale proved to be one of the most challenging aspects of the project. The density of the site plan meant that dozens of details—from the location of mailboxes and trash enclosures to HVAC condensing units—involved extensive negotiations and several zoning variances, along with a rigorous design review process, to win final approvals for the project. Shortridge was able to draw on his prior experience working through the approvals on similar projects in the Los Angeles area to navigate through this process, securing final approval in late 2016.

Construction on the Lomita project commenced in the fall of 2017 and continued through the summer of 2019. The rear units were framed first, followed by the four units at the street. Once all the units were framed, the balance of work on all six units proceeded synchronously.

According to Jack Masterson, Project Manager for Construction with SGV Habitat, the majority of the project was constructed with the affiliate's normal blend of volunteers, experienced affiliate construction staff, and subcontracted professionals. A few details, like aspects of the fire separation details at the party walls and the membrane roofing, were new to the affiliate. Masterson reported that the complexity of the units' overall form and exterior siding details contributed to about a 9% higher cost per unit for the project than comparable affiliate projects built in the same timeframe.

Key Lessons

One of the most important lessons of the Lomita Avenue project was the importance of working through the negotiations with city officials to achieve the desired project outcomes. "It's not uncommon for a young firm that doesn't have a lot of experience [with this aspect of the process] to take on a Habitat project," Shortridge said. "But they don't have the experience to know when to push back." In his view, architects too often accept whatever the city asks for rather than exploring options that the officials might ultimately accept.

The complexity of the approvals path for the Lomita Avenue project and the need to achieve higher-density outcomes represents a common challenge for urban-based Habitat for Humanity affiliates. Over four years passed from the initial agreement with the City of Glendale to homeowner move-in. Land values in Glendale also meant that the design team and the affiliate had to get as many units as possible on the site, requiring a more expensive type of construction. According to Yates, these pressures have pushed SGV Habitat to pull back from building in places like Glendale in favor of more suburban communities in the San Gabriel Valley, where project approvals are less arduous and lower-density construction is possible.

Lomita Avenue Townhomes site plan

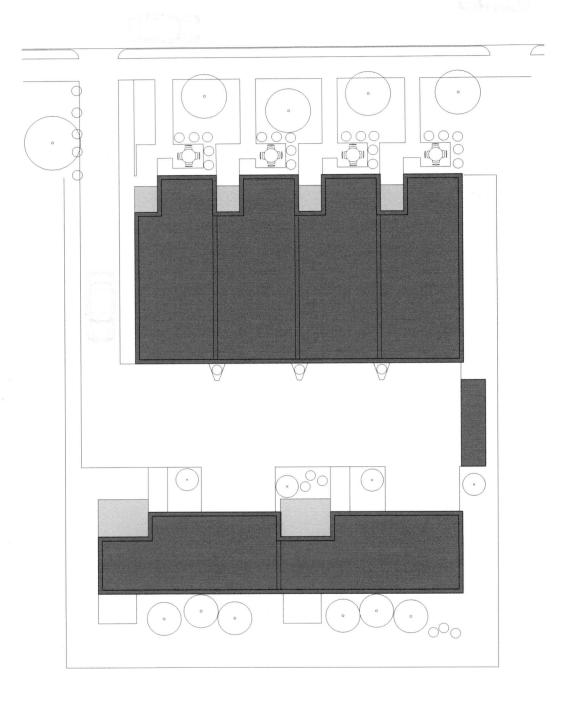

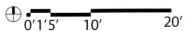

Lomita Avenue Townhomes floor plans (on-street units above, rear units below)

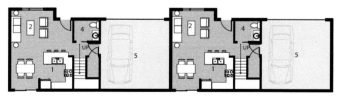

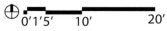

1 Kitchen
2 Living Room
3 Bedroom
4 Bathroom
5 Garage

LOMITA AVENUE TOWNHOMES

Aerial view of the project

View of units along Lomita Avenue

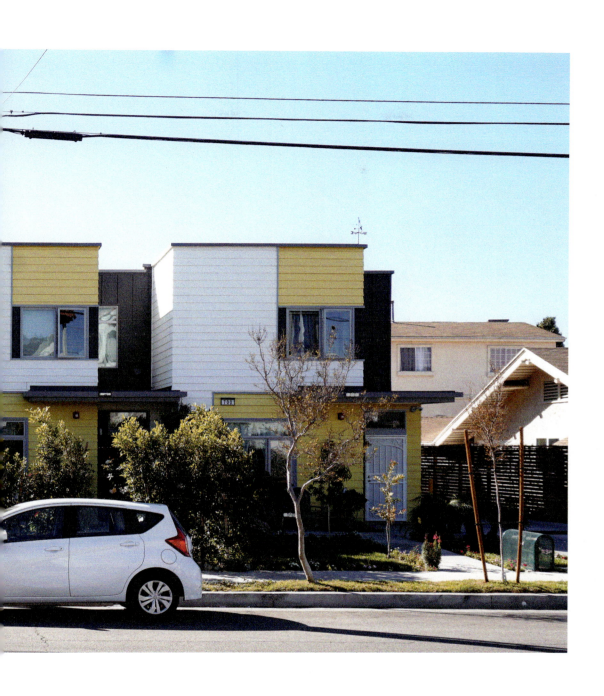

View of a Lomita Avenue unit entrance

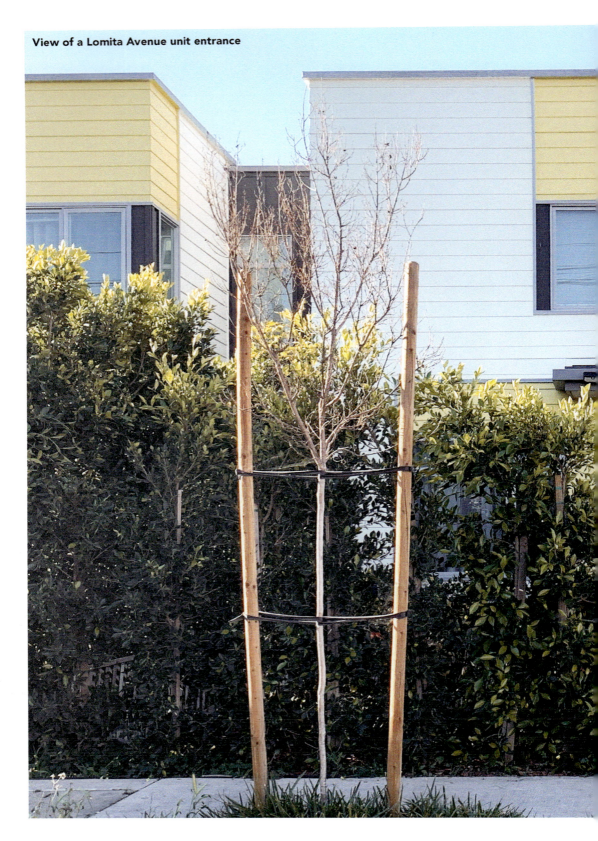

View of the entrance to the courtyard with a rear unit beyond

View of a rear unit entrance

130   LOMITA AVENUE TOWNHOMES

Chapter 10

Mueller Row Townhomes

Austin, Texas

Austin Habitat for Humanity® and Michael Hsu Office of Architecture

Key Partnerships

Phyllis Snodgrass (Executive Director) and Greg Anderson, Austin Habitat for Humanity

Michael Hsu (Principal) and Ken Johnson (Principal-in-Charge), Michael Hsu Office of Architecture

Project Summary

Master planned neighborhood context

11-unit townhome development

Nine 3-bedroom units

1,220 square feet

Two 4-bedroom, 2.5-bath units

1,452 square feet

Project Overview

The Mueller Row Townhomes were a collaboration between Austin Habitat for Humanity and Michael Hsu Office of Architecture. Located in the Mueller master planned community in Austin, Texas, the Mueller Row Townhomes were a breakthrough project for Austin Habitat—elevating the community perception of the design quality an affiliate could complete and opening new opportunities for collaborations within the local housing development community.[1]

DOI: 10.4324/9781003253501-10

Design Process

Located on the former site of the Austin airport, Mueller is a 700-acre, mixed-use master planned community developed via a partnership between the City of Austin and Catellus Development Corporation (Catellus). The development includes over 10,000 units of housing, 25 percent of which are earmarked for affordable homes. Austin Habitat for Humanity (Austin Habitat) had been negotiating with Catellus for the opportunity to build in Mueller, and in early 2018, they were offered the opportunity to develop a 15,500-square foot parcel.

Knowing that development on the Mueller site would be subject to the development's rigorous design review, Austin Habitat issued a request for proposals to the best architects in Austin. Austin Habitat selected Michael Hsu Office of Architecture, an award-winning design firm with a portfolio of innovative housing projects in Texas and around the country, including projects in Mueller. According to Michael Hsu, founding principal of his eponymous firm, the staff of the office had been looking for an opportunity to work on an innovative, affordable housing project. They knew that the Mueller site would help Austin Habitat develop a new project type—one that would require a creative response due to the image and character standards of the development.

The parcel offered to Habitat Austin allowed for higher density than other areas of Austin. This presented an opportunity to configure the Mueller Row design in a unique way. The townhomes were organized as two four-home clusters flanking a three-home unit. Nine of the 11 homes were three-bedroom units, with the homes at each end of the block configured as four-bedroom units. Each unit was two stories with parking in the rear of the units. The front yards of the townhomes included a sidewalk and bikeway, and they faced a community park across the street. The lower level contained the living, dining, and kitchen spaces. Four bedrooms and two full baths made up the upper level on the outside clusters, with three bedrooms and two full baths making up the upper level at the middle cluster.

The exterior massing featured small shifts between adjacent units, giving each unit different expressions within the clusters. They also used

MUELLER ROW TOWNHOMES 133

the exterior cladding palettes for variation: brick, fiber cement configured as panels, and fiber cement in a board-and-batten pattern.

For Hsu and Ken Johnson, Principal-in-Charge for the Mueller Row project, the design for Mueller Row evolved via a series of collaborative design sessions involving several architects in the office. Most of the office's projects have high-end materials and generous budgets. Hsu and his colleagues approached the design of the Mueller Row Townhomes with the same design effort they bring to all their work despite the modest budget of the project. For Hsu, this meant his staff had to find ways to get the most mileage out of modest design ideas, balancing budget and creativity at every turn. For example, in one of the bedrooms facing the street, the team used a window that was a foot taller than all the others—positioned between roof trusses—to bring more light into the room while creating a subtle shift in rhythm on the exterior facades. In another example, small shifts in the brick pattern brought design interest to the facades.

The architects also reached out to their contacts in the local construction community to secure in-kind material donations. One of the most impactful gifts was the tile used as an accent panel at the recessed entrance of each unit. The bold color and pattern of the tile contrasted with the neutral colors of the rest of the building and drew attention to the entry porches.

Billy Whipple, Austin Habitat's Senior Vice President for Construction, also played a critical role in the design process for Mueller Row. Whipple had experience in commercial construction prior to joining Austin Habitat, and according to Phyllis Snodgrass, Executive Director of Austin Habitat, and Hsu, his depth of expertise was invaluable. From the outset of the project, Austin Habitat made it clear that they hoped to replicate the design approach for Mueller Row on other sites. Whipple worked closely with the architects to refine the design and reconcile the budget. He was particularly focused on adapting details to be completed easily by volunteers.

Snodgrass credited the balance of design quality and affordability to the give-and-take between the architects and Whipple. "We really put [the architects] through the wringer regarding the budget, but that constraint made them think differently. I think they really appreciated it in the end," Snodgrass said.

Construction Process

Unexpected delays related to the transfer of the land title to the affiliate held the project up for over 10 months, and permit reviews pushed the construction start into the spring of 2020.

While Austin Habitat acted as the general contractor on the project, the constraints of the COVID-19 pandemic, the newness of the details associated with the townhouse typology, and Catellus's schedule expectations led the affiliate to subcontract most of the construction rather than depend on community volunteers as much as they commonly did. The focus of the Austin Habitat construction team shifted from coordinating community volunteers to managing the subcontractor team and the construction schedule. "We wanted to get in and out smoothly and demonstrate that we could complete this type of project successfully," Snodgrass said.

The experience and professionalism of Austin Habitat's construction staff impressed Johnson, in particular their incorporation of project management software and the effectiveness of their project communications. "[The construction] was faster than what we see in market-rate housing construction. They ran a very tight ship." Construction at Mueller Row was completed in the spring of 2021, and the new homeowners moved in during early summer.

Key Lessons

Snodgrass was excited about the potential of replicating Mueller Row's townhome typology on future sites. The affiliate's construction staff have gained valuable experience regarding the details associated with townhome construction—such as party walls and fire-resistant assemblies—and the time invested in working with the architects to make these details volunteer friendly is beginning to pay off. "This was really good training for our team," Snodgrass said. "I'm sure we're going to be repeating this type of project."

Hsu and Johnson were pleased with the effect working on Mueller Row had on their staff as well. The opportunity to apply the firm's design experience and creativity on a project with a modest budget was a great learning experience for younger staff members. "This project allowed us to flex different muscles. It was really fun," Hsu said.

The City of Austin has ambitious goals for the development of affordable housing and requires almost all market-rate projects to include affordable units. One of Austin Habitat's main objectives for Mueller Row was to demonstrate to the city's development community that it could create affordable housing that was compatible with these developments. For Snodgrass, Mueller Row was a tremendous success in this regard, changing perceptions of the affiliate and opening doors across Austin. "We've had several developers who we've been negotiating with for years call us after seeing Mueller Row and say, 'Wow, we need to talk.' Suddenly we have their attention."

The way Mueller Row influenced community perceptions regarding the character of affordable housing—in addition to the resulting opportunities for Austin Habitat—is one of the most gratifying outcomes of the collaboration for Hsu. "That makes us feel really good," he said. "The city needs more projects like this."

Mueller Row Townhomes site plan

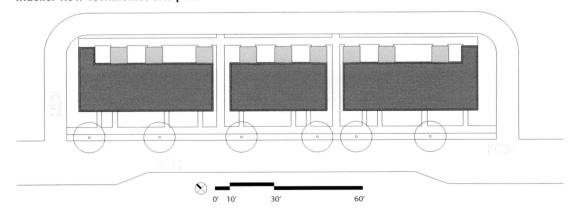

Mueller Row Townhomes, three- and four-bedroom unit floor plans

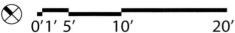

1 Kitchen
2 Living Room
3 Bedroom
4 Bathroom
5 Entry Porch
6 Rear Porch
7 Carport

View of the townhomes from the street

138 MUELLER ROW TOWNHOMES

MUELLER ROW TOWNHOMES   139

View of the townhomes with adjacent market-rate projects beyond

MUELLER ROW TOWNHOMES 141

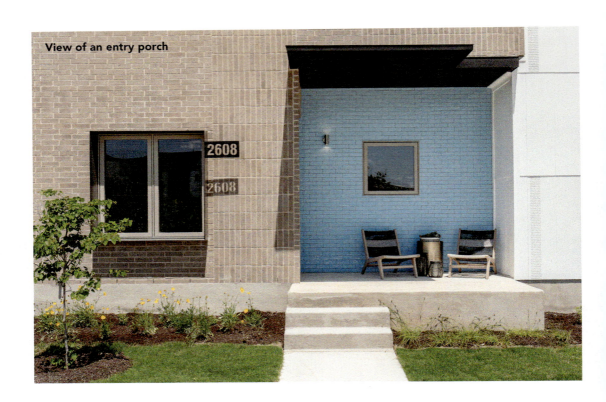

View of an entry porch

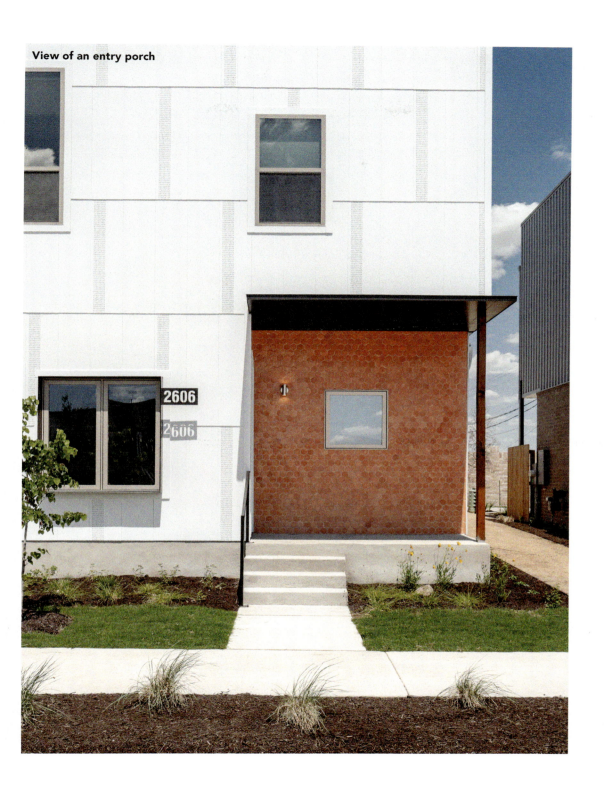

View of an entry porch

MUELLER ROW TOWNHOMES 143

View of a townhome unit showing tile and masonry patterns

View of a porch through the front entry

View of a covered porch at the rear of a unit

View of a bedroom showing tall window detail

Chapter 11

Oxford Green

Philadelphia, Pennsylvania
Habitat for Humanity® Philadelphia and ISA

Key Partnerships

Brian Phillips (Principal), ISA

K.C. Roney (Executive Director) and Tya Winn, Habitat for Humanity Philadelphia

Program Summary

Urban neighborhood context

Twenty 3-bedroom, 2.5-bath single-family row houses

1,700 square feet (including unfinished basement)

Project Overview

Oxford Green is a 20-unit row house development developed via a collaboration between Habitat for Humanity Philadelphia and ISA. The project is located in the Sharswood neighborhood of northwest Philadelphia, forming the northern edge of a Choice Neighborhoods redevelopment site. The three-story rowhouse units reflect a contemporary interpretation of the city's iconic row house typology with a floor plan designed to allow homeowners multiple ways to configure the main level. Oxford Green was the largest redevelopment project completed by Habitat Philadelphia, significantly expanding the affiliate's capacity to manage larger-scale projects.[1]

DOI: 10.4324/9781003253501-11

Preconstruction Process

In 2011, the City of Philadelphia began working with residents of the Sharswood neighborhood, located northwest of Center City Philadelphia, on strategies for addressing the critical problems residents face. The Philadelphia Housing Authority's (PHA's) Blumberg Apartments, built on an eight-acre site in Sharswood in 1966, had become a symbol of highly concentrated poverty and criminality.[2] While the neighborhoods around Sharswood were seeing new development, the high concentration of high-rise public housing and the negative impact of public safety concerns in the area made it an island of deep and sustained poverty, vacant lots, and abandoned homes.

Beginning in 2013, with support from the US Department of Housing and Urban Development's Choice Neighborhoods program, the PHA and the City of Philadelphia began work on a comprehensive transformation plan for Sharswood. Completed in 2015, the resulting plan included measures for education, health and wellness, workforce and small business development, green infrastructure, and access to social services and public safety measures. The housing component of the plan centered on demolishing most of the Blumberg Apartment complex and partnering with private and nonprofit developers to build over 500 new rental housing units and 68 affordable homeownership units. The plan also called for an extensive program of repairs and improvements intended to stabilize the existing housing stock in Sharswood, most of which were row houses built in the late 19th century.

As the Choice Neighborhoods Plan was developed, PHA sought out an implementation partner for two blocks (approximately 32,000 square feet) on Oxford Street that were master planned for homeownership row houses. Holding the northern edge of the Blumberg site, the Oxford Street site faced one of the most intact blocks of existing homes and would serve as a buffer between the homeownership and rental sections of the redeveloped area. According to Tya Winn, PHA's Program Manager at the time, PHA needed a housing builder and developer who could deliver

OXFORD GREEN 149

quality homes quickly and in a way that generated community support for the entire plan.

Habitat for Humanity Philadelphia (Philadelphia Habitat) was, in many ways, a natural partner for PHA. Active since 1985, Philadelphia Habitat had strong community support and a reputation for successful affordable housing development across the city. Philadelphia Habitat's Executive Director K.C. Roney characterized the affiliate as "the best game in town when it comes to affordable housing." Philadelphia Habitat had been involved in the planning stages of the Choice Neighborhoods process in Sharswood and had begun working with PHA on the home repair component of the plan.

The Oxford Street parcels presented a tantalizing opportunity to develop 20 homes—the largest single-site opportunity the affiliate had ever encountered. "Habitat became the natural partner," Winn said. "They were an easy win from the Housing Authority's viewpoint. They could build faster than a government agency, and they're focused on homeownership. Who's going to object to Habitat?"

In 2019, Philadelphia Habitat signed a memorandum of agreement with PHA for 20 parcels along Oxford Street—nine in the east block and 11 in the west. The agreement included partial funding for the new homes as well as design standards developed by PHA and deadlines for completion. Just after the agreement with PHA, Winn joined Philadelphia Habitat as Director of Project Planning and Design and assumed responsibility for the Oxford Street project, which was later christened Oxford Green by the homeowners.

Oxford Green held many firsts for the affiliate: design and implementation negotiations with PHA, street improvements, and navigation of the city's new stormwater management regulations. The affiliate would also have to secure the entirety of the project's $7 million funding before PHA would transfer the land title. "Everything was new all of a sudden," Winn said. "We had to start looking like a real developer."

Winn's first task was to hire a design team. She issued a request for proposals sourcing design services from several architects based in Philadelphia, some of whom had prior experience with Philadelphia Habitat. Brian Phillips, Principal at ISA and design lead on Oxford Green, said that the firm's research on previous Philadelphia Habitat models contributed toward its selection. In his view, the project provided a great opportunity to reinterpret aspects of the iconic row house typology and examine some of the affiliate's standard construction details.

Design Process

Several key issues emerged in the initial design stages of the project: How could the layout accommodate multiple-family structures and aging in place? How would the project adapt to the city's stormwater management requirements? How would the project's facades respond to the surrounding urban context and the PHA design standards?

The Oxford Green units feature a living room, kitchen, bathroom, and dining space on the ground floor, plus three bedrooms and a bathroom on the second floor. Additionally, each home contains an unfinished basement for future build out or storage. ISA proposed moving the kitchen from the rear of the main level to the middle of the plan, allowing each homeowner the option to create a ground floor bedroom or home office in the future. "Seeing how the homeowners have used that space has been really cool," Roney said. "They've come up with iterations we hadn't even contemplated." This adjustment also aligned the kitchen under the second level bathroom, unlocking efficiencies in plumbing and other construction systems.

An in-kind donation of prefabricated kitchen cabinet systems led to another opportunity to give homeowners options for the interiors of the homes. ISA and Philadelphia Habitat developed two color palettes: dark cabinets with light finished wood flooring and light cabinets with a dark finish on the floors. Homeowners could choose their preferred palette when selecting their unit.

The city's stormwater management rules mandated that 90 percent of rainwater be retained onsite. Typically, urban sites use a large underground stormwater basin, but that would require the homeowners to share responsibility for maintaining that system. To avoid this condition, the team installed green roofs—another first for Philadelphia Habitat—that allowed each home to function as a separate system. The affiliate was careful to work with the installer to ensure that these systems could be maintained by the homeowners and easily serviced.

The existing row houses in the Sharswood neighborhood featured a rich and diverse mix of color and pattern, and one of PHA's key design standards called for the new homes to relate to this content in a sensitive way. In Phillips's view, translating the ornate and detailed facades of the existing row houses into the more affordable fiber cement material palette presented one of the most challenging aspects of the project. ISA analyzed the components of these homes and developed the design vocabulary around details and materials that were familiar to Philadelphia Habitat and could be built without skilled labor. The resulting facades used a palette of repeating elements arrayed with shifts in pattern and color to give each home a unique treatment.

The apparent complexity of the facades raised concerns within the affiliate, so the team built a full-scale mockup of a typical street facade in the affiliate's warehouse, which proved to be a pivotal step in gaining support for the design. Working out the various details via the mockup gave the architects and the affiliate staff confidence that the design approach would be successful. ISA used its connections with material suppliers to secure significant in-kind donations, allowing the affiliate to upgrade the material approach to the whole exterior.

Construction Process

Resolving the stormwater management plan and navigating approvals from the city delayed the construction start of the project until spring of 2019. Dale Corporation, one of the area's largest builders, agreed to frame all 20 homes, allowing Philadelphia Habitat to make up for some of this delay. Despite the outbreak of the COVID-19 pandemic in the spring of 2020, construction activities at Oxford Green were allowed to continue. Ironically, the slowdown in the larger construction economy benefited the Oxford Green project, as it freed up busy contractors. Dale Corporation, for example, was able to commit a full framing crew to the project and framed the first block of nine homes in a few months. The first nine homes were completed in the fall of 2020, and the second block was completed in the summer of 2021.

Key Lessons

According to Winn, the scale and pace of the construction at Oxford Green pushed Philadelphia Habitat to adopt new approaches to managing the construction process. "We are an affiliate with over 20 years of construction experience, but we did not really see ourselves as a real construction company, as a real affordable housing developer," Winn said. However, as the project progressed, the project team adopted more sophisticated project management practices, including detailed schedule planning, formalized project specifications, and a heightened focus on communication across the team. These process and collaboration advancements—as well as an innovative design—contributed to the project's recognition: an award from Habitat for Humanity International for Equity of Design in 2021, a 2021 Merit Award from AIA Pennsylvania, and an 2021 AIA Tri-State Honor Award.

The scale and pace of the project also led Philadelphia Habitat to adjust its approach to the role of unskilled volunteers in the construction of Oxford Green and rely more heavily on professional subcontractors than it had in the past.

Completing Oxford Green transformed Philadelphia Habitat. Taking on a project of this scale and complexity cemented the affiliate's role as one of the most experienced and capable affordable housing builder-developers in the region. "We liked to see ourselves as a group of ragtag, holistic, Christian volunteers," Winn said. "But we had to accept that we're a real construction company and a real development company." Navigating the complexities of working with PHA and the city's engineering departments—as well as incorporating more professional subcontractors—challenged the affiliate's capacities and, in Winn's view, significantly increased Philadelphia Habitat's capacity to manage future projects of this scale.

From Roney's perspective, seeing the scale of impact the affiliate had by concentrating such a broad scope of initiatives on a single district was one of the most significant outcomes of Oxford Green. In her view, the extensive home repair program, neighborhood coalition building, and 20 new homes have had a positive combined effect on Sharswood. "We want to cluster our impact in an area and offer all the services we can," Roney said. "Our goal is to provide Habitat homeowners with safe, warm, and dry homes, but if they walk out their door and like what they see, they're more likely to want to stay there."

The opportunity to work with a mission-driven client like Philadelphia Habitat struck a resonant chord with Phillips. "To be stewards of design in service of affordable housing is amazing. [Partnering with Habitat] is a peerless way to bring architects into contact with homeowners who never get the opportunity to experience buildings designed by architects." While Habitat affiliates must manage all the constraints that other affordable housing developers do, they have more space in their process to think meaningfully about the impact of design. "I think it's a more human-centered process than what you'll see from a more institutional affordable housing developer," he said.

Several aspects of the Oxford Green design have been carried over into Philadelphia Habitat's current and future work, including the configuration of the main level plan. Moving the kitchen from the back of the plan to the middle opened a wide range of options for homeowners, a feature the affiliate plans to utilize in future projects. Philadelphia Habitat has also adopted ISA's approach to fiber cement siding for a fresh take on the volunteer-friendly material.

In Roney's view, Oxford Green also helped the affiliate build and refine its capacity to successfully partner with material donors, construction professionals, and public agencies—which significantly enhanced the affiliate's ability to take on more challenging and complex projects.

Oxford Green site plan

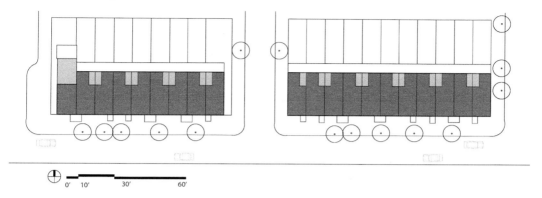

Oxford Green floor plans

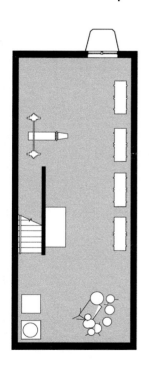
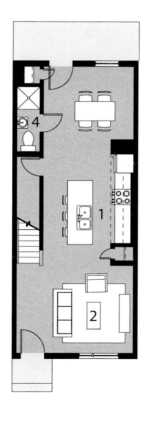
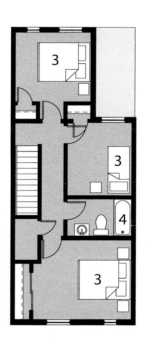

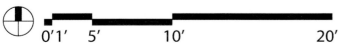

1 Kitchen
2 Living Room
3 Bedroom
4 Bathroom

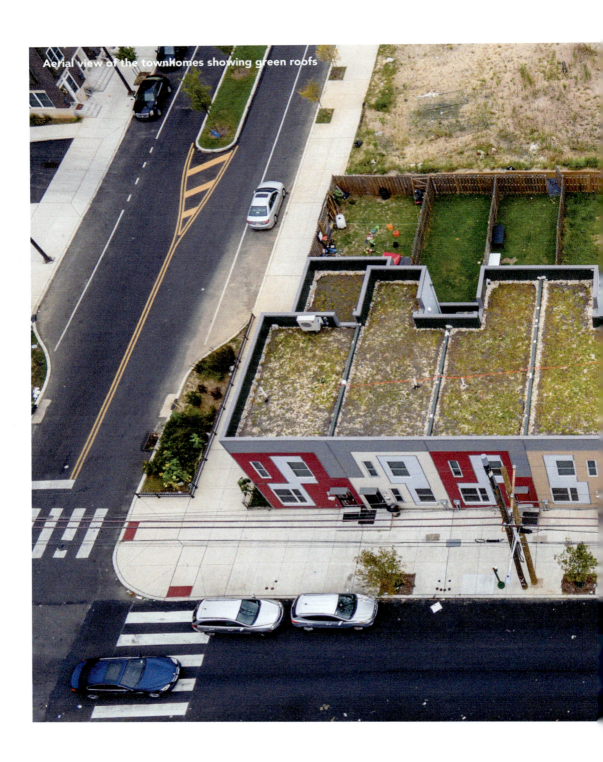

Aerial view of the townhomes showing green roofs

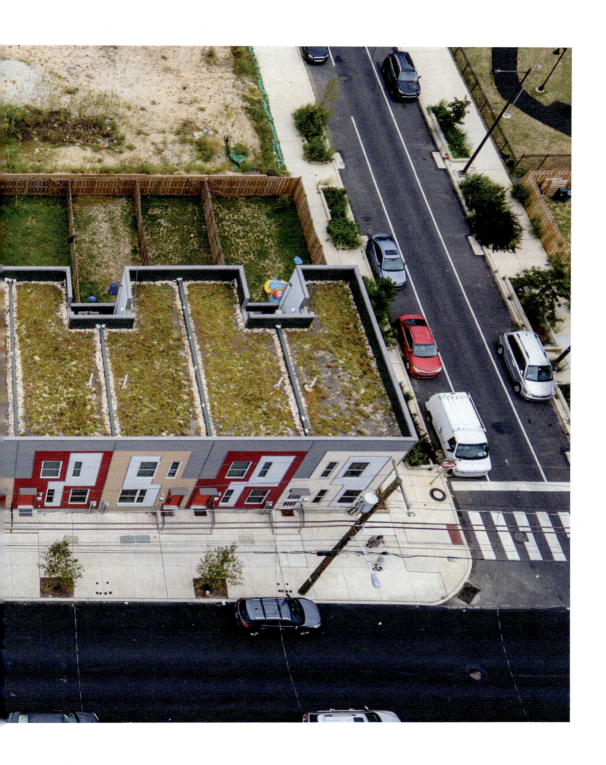

Street view showing adjacent existing homes

facade vocabulary analysis prepared by ISA

EXISTING PROTOTYPE
FACADE

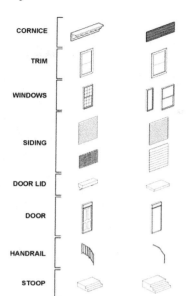

CORNICE
TRIM
WINDOWS
SIDING
DOOR LID
DOOR
HANDRAIL
STOOP

CONTEXTUALIZED
PROTOTYPE FACADE

OXFORD GREEN

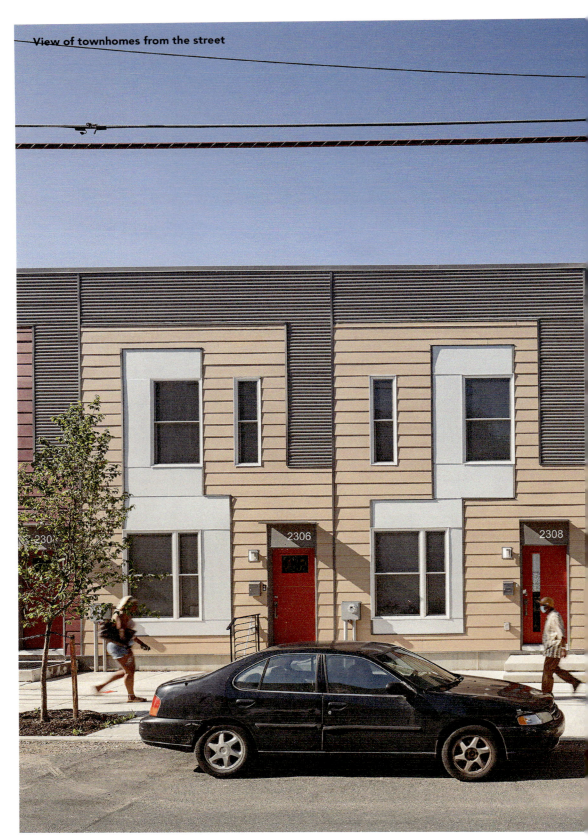
View of townhomes from the street

OXFORD GREEN 161

View of the kitchen in central position on the main level

View of the upper level corridor

Chapter 12

SEED Affordable Housing

Brownsville, Brooklyn, New York
Habitat for Humanity® New York City and Westchester County and LATENT Productions

Partnerships

Karen Haycox (Chief Executive Officer), Matt Dunbar (Chief Strategy Officer and Executive Vice President), Orlando Marin (Vice President, Real Estate and Construction), Juliana Bernal Guinand (Director of Real Estate Development), and Elizabeth Tietjen (Director of Marketing and Communications), Habitat for Humanity New York City and Westchester County

Karla Rothstein (Principal) and Salvatore Perry (Principal), LATENT Productions

Program Summary

25-unit affordable housing infill development

Three four-story walk-up buildings

Seven 1-bedroom, fifteen 2-bedroom, and three 3-bedroom apartments

39,000 square feet

Project Overview

SEED was a collaboration between LATENT Productions, a New York City–based architecture, research, and development firm; Habitat for Humanity New York City (Habitat NYC) and Westchester County (Habitat NYC); and the New York City Department of Housing Preservation & Development (NYC HPD). The project

DOI: 10.4324/9781003253501-12

developed out of the NYC HPD New Infill Homeownership Opportunities Program (NIHOP).[1] The project team navigated a series of regulatory checkpoints to realize the project as a co-op development. The project is the second largest that Habitat NYC has built to date.[2]

Design Process

In 2007, the NYC HPD NIHOP issued a competitive request for proposals (RFP) to develop a set of infill sites for affordable housing built to Enterprise Green Communities and EPA Energy Star Standards. Karla Rothstein, cofounder and Design Director of LATENT Productions, recalled when they reviewed the RFP, the team at LATENT Productions was intrigued by the fact that the project was identified as workforce housing aimed at providing individuals a piece of equity in the city. The program was also focused on developing homeownership opportunities in neighborhoods that had both infill lots available and a lack of opportunities for homeownership. LATENT Productions partnered with Adam Dayem of Actual/Office to develop a schematic proposal for a set of ten scattered infill sites in Brooklyn, New York. The sites the team selected were all the same dimension, opening up opportunities to think about the project as a series of modules, which supported the project's affordability. LATENT Productions's proposal was successful, and the firm was designated as the developer for the project.

However, the designated sites were not the modular, level, and consistently sized parcels of their proposal. Instead, the team was allotted five long vacant parcels that were each unique, irregularly shaped, and sloped. The sites, located in Brownsville, Brooklyn, fronted two streets and included a corner lot. This configuration led the team to identify two key opportunities for the design. The first was the opportunity to reassert the urban street wall, develop the corner, and create a strong presence for the project within the neighborhood. The second opportunity was to create a shared courtyard within the block that connected the five parcels and negotiated the topographic change across the site.

SEED AFFORDABLE HOUSING   165

As a result of the parcel locations, the project was designed as three 4-story walk-up buildings. Salvatore Perry, cofounder and Development Director of LATENT Productions, and Rothstein recalled that an important aspect of the project was reconstituting the urban block and establishing a cohesive presence for the project that was something more than a series of individual buildings. The team worked with the city to navigate the design through the Uniform Land Use Review Process (ULURP). Through this process, the team was able to get the city to re-plat the five parcels into three, which allowed for the development of the 25-unit project.

Within the three building volumes, the team ensured the buildings were legible as a singular design. The design team utilized a concrete panel rainscreen facade to unify all three buildings by establishing a common facade materiality. Projecting box-bay windows punctuated the facade and gave the building a strong identity within the urban context.

The shared courtyard's connection to the street and units drove design decisions. While reestablishing the street wall was a priority, the team did not want the design to be entirely insular or fortress-like. A shared laundry facility community room on the ground floor opened onto the planted courtyard. Large-scale openings in the building facade offer views from the sidewalk into the courtyard. These openings provided both direct and visual connections through the building and created a more engaging ground floor experience.

From the outset, attention was given to ensuring that the spaces had copious natural light, ventilation and connection to social spaces. The living spaces were organized facing the courtyard so that the daily life inside the apartments overlooked the shared community space. Similarly, the location of the stairwells on the courtyard allowed for daylit vertical movement to activate the interior of the block. While the stairwell's windows open into the courtyard and provide light and views, the most distinctive feature of the buildings are the projecting box-bay windows that face the street. The bay windows give the building both a presence in the city and additional space and light to each apartment.

166   SEED AFFORDABLE HOUSING

As the team at LATENT Productions worked through the design process with the community and NYC HPD, they were simultaneously working with consultants at Steven Winter Associates to identify systems and assemblies necessary to meet EPA Energy Star and Enterprise Green Community standards—to ensure that the costs to maintain homeownership would continue to be affordable for residents into the future. With the design nearing completion, the team was preparing to move forward when the market crashed in 2008. Rothstein recalled that the financial crisis shifted the city's focus from new construction to rehab and renovation projects; SEED was put on hold.

Catalysts for Collaboration

In 2014, the city's policy had shifted, and the NYC HPD returned part of its focus to new construction projects. In the intervening period, project financing models changed across the residential sector, and a collaboration emerged in 2015 between Habitat NYC and LATENT Productions to codevelop SEED.

Karen Haycox, Habitat NYC's Chief Executive Officer, noted that the opportunity enabled the affiliate to remain true to the Habitat mission of providing affordable homeownership to low- and moderate-income New Yorkers and to do so at a greater scale. The affiliate had also committed to preserving the affordability of the housing created in service to future generations of low-income New Yorkers using a range of development strategies. For SEED, Habitat NYC shifted from developing condominiums to developing co-op units, a tactic that provided the opportunity to both reach lower-income populations and preserve affordable housing for future generations. The Habitat NYC team admitted this was a significant change and had substantial and positive long-term implications for the project.

The LATENT Productions team supported this idea, and the project began navigation of the City's ULURP process, which involved presentations to and approval from community boards, the borough president, and the mayor's office. Prior to approaching the city, the team reviewed the mix of unit types and sizes for the building. Perry recalled that Habitat NYC sought to increase the number of three-bedroom units that could house larger or multigenerational families. LATENT Productions was able to alter the unit mix slightly while maintaining the building's overall design intent.

Matt Dunbar, Habitat NYC's Chief Strategy Officer and Executive Vice President, reiterated the importance of this step, as sites designated for infill development often exist within disinvested neighborhoods. The prospect of offering homeownership opportunities to residents who had grown up in the neighborhood is always a primary focus of the affiliate. Offering a diversity of unit types in an affordable ownership project provides more options for the neighborhood and future residents of varying family sizes, and it positively impacts the neighborhood as a whole.

Habitat NYC elected to pursue a co-op model (versus their previously preferred condo approach) which, while limiting the amount of equity gained by the family at the sale of a unit, assisted in the goal of preserving the unit in perpetuity and deepened the impact of the public investment in SEED. The project also sought local political support for the 40-year tax exemption—renewable for an additional 40-year term—in order to support long-term affordability goals. Without these strategies, Orlando Marin, Habitat NYC's Vice President of Real Estate and Construction, suggested that the units are at risk of being lost to the market.

LATENT Productions had successfully navigated the rezoning process for the site to be developed as a condominium project before the project was put on hold. As the team settled on a new mix of unit types, they returned to the rezoning process to shift from condominiums to co-op development. The team needed to return to the local city council member and community to seek approval for the change. Habitat and LATENT Productions entered into this process during the city council's local election cycle. A newly elected council member favored the change and supported the team's request to develop the project as a co-op. Then, the team moved forward to the construction phase, breaking ground on the project in 2017.

Construction Process

SEED received financing through several programs under the Housing New York plan implemented during Mayor Bill de Blasio's term.[3] NYC HPD's NIHOP and the New York Housing and Community Renewal provided $11 million in project funding.[4] A partnership between Community Preservation Corporation and the Goldman Sachs Urban Investment Group provided the project with a $2.86 million construction loan.[5]

As Perry recalled, the team at Habitat NYC was open to and supportive of the design direction prior to their involvement on the project. The design offered Habitat NYC an opportunity to "push the envelope and to provide a different and more modern option for homeowners," said Juliana Bernal Guinand, Habitat NYC's Director of Real Estate Development. Guinand noted that this approach extended from interior to exterior.

The unit interiors are minimal and more modern in terms of materials and finishes. LATENT Productions had designed the building utilizing precast hollow core concrete planks with exposed concrete ceilings and polished concrete floors. The Habitat NYC team was supportive of the efforts to maintain a material consistency and restraint across the project.

For Orlando Marin, the benefits were clear. The design incorporated many elements that contributed to homeowner wellness, such as the material palette's inherently low volatile organic compound levels and easy maintenance. The work that the LATENT Productions team had completed with energy consultant Steven Winter Associates provided units that were affordable in terms of anticipated utility costs. Additionally, the team's decisions to incorporate energy recovery ventilators, water-saving devices, and self-shading box-bay windows had a positive impact on the building's ability to meet those standards.

Key Lessons

The physical layout of SEED's site posed both opportunities and challenges that the team synthesized into a design that provided 25 affordable homes and filled vacant lots in the neighborhood. The project was also complex to develop, requiring expertise with an array of financial incentive programs. Salvatore Perry noted that Habitat NYC had a robust leadership team that was able to navigate several key financial subsidies for the project, providing funding sources that LATENT Productions would not have had access to on its own.

Haycox noted that the challenges of building in New York are driven, in large part, by rapidly escalating land costs. This caused the affiliate to develop areas of expertise within the organization, aligning Habitat NYC with large development companies in the area.

ED site plan

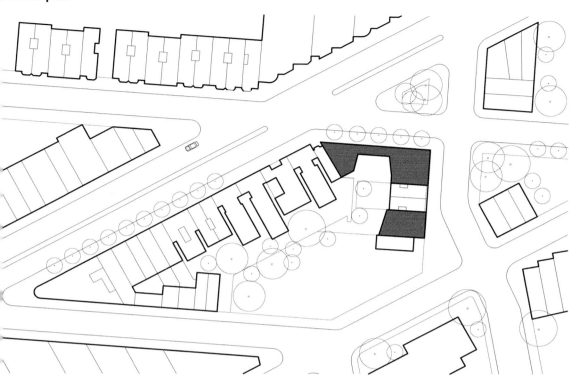

0' 50' 100'

SEED AFFORDABLE HOUSING   171

SEED ground level plan and typical upper level floor plan

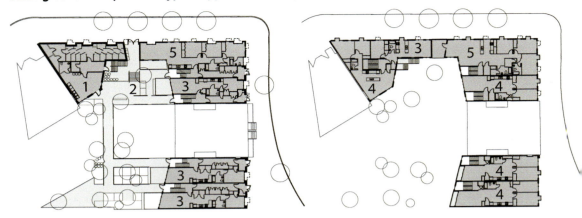

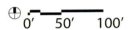

1 Shared Laundry and Bicycle Storage
2 Shared Courtyard
3 One-Bedroom Unit
4 Two-Bedroom Unit
5 Three-Bedroom Unit

View of SEED from the Eastern Parkway

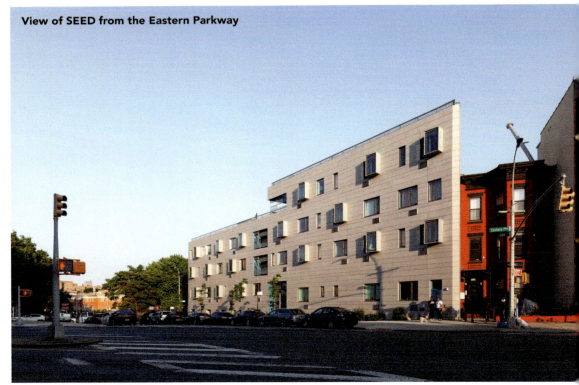

View of SEED from the intersection

SEED AFFORDABLE HOUSING

View of SEED from Thomas S Boyland Street

SEED AFFORDABLE HOUSING 175

View of the SEED courtyard

View of the north facade

View of the kitchen in an upper level unit

View of the living space in an upper level unit

View of box bay windows

SEED AFFORDABLE HOUSING

Chapter 13

A Conversation with Affiliate Leaders

DOI: 10.4324/9781003253501-13

The collaborations described in the preceding chapters chronicle innovative projects undertaken by Habitat for Humanity® affiliates and their design partners. This collection of projects reflects larger changes that have occurred within affiliates across the country over the past decade. Several past and present affiliate leaders were invited to discuss the case studies' major themes and provide insight into the contours of the changing affordable housing landscape. The panel session was organized around three main themes: new approaches to building, affiliate organization and culture, and partnerships with architects.[1]

Panel

> Phyllis Snodgrass, Chief Executive Officer, Austin Habitat for Humanity
>
> Billy Whipple, Senior Vice President of Construction, Austin Habitat for Humanity
>
> Karen Haycox, Chief Executive Officer, Habitat for Humanity New York City and Westchester County
>
> Marty Kooistra, Black Home Initiative Project Manager at Civic Commons (Center for Community Investment) and former CEO of Habitat for Humanity Seattle–King and Kittitas Counties
>
> Tya Winn, Executive Director of the Community Design Collaborative and former Director of Project Planning and Design for Habitat for Humanity Philadelphia

When we started researching projects for *Designed for Habitat: New Directions for Habitat for Humanity* 11 years ago, an emerging priority was to balance optimizing first costs (initial construction) and long-term operating costs (primarily energy) of the home.

We've observed a large shift between the sets of interviews we did for the first book (in 2012), and those for this book. It seems now that many Habitat affiliates have embraced this shift, and we

have heard many different approaches to addressing operating costs versus first costs.

Marty Kooistra

This remains one of the interesting tensions in the affordable housing world. For me, trying to blend those tensions of first cost, the climate crisis, and the affordability crisis has been a lifelong mission. One of the pivotal moments at Habitat for Humanity International was when we were able to secure the $30+ million contribution from Home Depot.[2] That contribution was designed to help affiliates scale up in terms of their sustainability standards. By removing the incremental first cost argument, you can move the culture much more quickly.

That said, this topic is both a societal problem and a communication issue, in many respects. If we can deal with the upfront costs, it is fewer dollars over the lifespan of a building, so it's more of an investment than an expense. The most important thing is thinking about how we balance that tension; get more product on the ground as quickly as we can; and make it a high-quality, highly sustainable product that a family can thrive in.

Tya Winn

I think it's complicated—at least I can speak for what I saw in Philadelphia and surrounding affiliates where we had close relationships. We had to get that first cost down, because we're not lowering the cost of the house, but subsidizing it. An upfront subsidy was necessary to make housing affordable—especially in cities where house prices were rising—for Habitat homeowners.

Billy Whipple

Going back to your comment about 11 years ago, 2009 was the first real implementation of the International Energy Conservation Code (IECC). That was when you began to see the IECC 2009 enter state, county, and municipal code requirements. However, our city funding is contingent on participating in a program that requires Austin Energy Green Building rating.[3] With both, we started just as high as we had too, and we were rather good at it. We run our energy efficiency strategy right down the middle of all the programs to accommodate USGBC LEED, Energy Star, Phius, and Austin Energy Green Building. Our building performance program is designed so we can pivot in any direction fairly easily—we're not turning down funding opportunities. And for us, the question has become, "What do we invest in?"

We focus heavily on the high barrier upgrade items with our budget, such as insulation, windows, foundations, and HVAC systems. We try to make sure that they have a good lifecycle. If somebody wants a nicer countertop or a nicer chandelier, that's a low-barrier item to replace, but solid wood cabinets are a lot more difficult. So we focus on items that a homeowner cannot upgrade more easily. It's a risk-versus-reward situation, and our interest is in protecting what the homeowner is going to have long term.

One of the things that we noted between our first book and our second is that, in places like Philadelphia and other large cities, this shift from a single-family home on its own lot with a front and backyard was already determined by the context. In this round of interviews, we've seen affiliates in places like Austin, Colorado, and Vermont shifting to higher-density housing typologies, as well as different approaches to site design where tight clusters of homes are becoming more common. We are interested in hearing from all of you about how that shift has influenced your affiliate.

Phyllis Snodgrass

We moved to that scale of development because the land available for single-family construction is just not close to work centers [in Austin]. The urban part of our region has gotten astronomically more expensive, and places where we used to purchase a lot for $5,000–$20,000 are now upwards of $100,000–$200,000. So, if you are going to find land anywhere near where someone works, you're either going to be in a special program that the city has carved out—which doesn't happen very often for us—or you found something you can infill and are able to do a more dense project.

Even with that, there's not a lot of availability. Our market has been so strong and so hot that the [for-profit] builders will take anything and everything. It's so expensive that the numbers don't always make sense, but we're pushing into it anyway. As we continue to find land, we can build some single-family homes because there is a market for that and there are people who really want it. We're also trying to build closer into the city.

Karen Haycox

We're in the high-density business [in New York] and have been for quite some time. We also do single-family housing; most of it is gut-rehab on older housing stock that comes to us through partnerships.

What we really look at are the community assets. We've been very focused on the other end of the continuum—how can we preserve the existing aging housing stock? In New York City in particular, there are a lot of existing co-ops that we work on preserving. If we don't, then we'll lose that housing stock to the market. We've developed and adapted our programs to serve and preserve co-ops. We work with the constituents in the building, identify their needs, renovate their facilities, and find new capital sources to do so.

We're also looking at a transition strategy where we can take rent-stabilized buildings and translate them into homeownership over 15 years, as well as developing rental buildings that will transition to homeownership using Low-Income Housing Tax Credit as a funding source. We're working to increase the marketability of our high-density projects, hold them long term, and find new ways to add to that density. We're looking at accessory dwelling units, which are being embraced around the country as a type used to increase density in existing neighborhoods. However, we're waiting for the governments to catch up and make it doable rather than academic.

Marty Kooistra

There hasn't been room here in the Seattle market for a single-family detached product. Going back to 2008 when I moved out here, we've been doing multiunit structures unless we're doing a preservation project. Finding a piece of land that is buildable and affordable is hard.

The entire historical community engagement model of Habitat is predicated on the construction of a single-family, detached, site-framed house. That is how everything got jazzed. When you talk to donors on Habitat boards, they go back to their original Habitat volunteer experience. So, pivoting the culture has always been hard.

We have also seen a shift toward the construction of multifamily buildings. Some of you have been building at this scale for some time now, and we are interested to hear more about how you approach this scale of construction. How are you adapting the role of community volunteers and homeowners in the construction of more complex building types, and how are you evaluating and incorporating Habitat's traditional volunteer labor in the process?

Billy Whipple

It's something that we wrestle with every single time we look at a piece of property. Our Vice President of Real Estate sends me a piece of property, and I look at it through multiple lenses as to what we can do. Liability is where the lines are drawn. If it's a product type that we can self-perform—which stays within light frame construction—we can build that with volunteers all day long.

Our production builders don't run out there and start a three-over-one condo building—that's a different company. So, if we can still perform it, then I can à la carte the volunteers where they add the most value. Once we are not able to self-perform from a management, insurance, or liability standpoint; that's where the wall goes up before volunteers touch it.

Otherwise, you start stepping into a commercial construction methodology where we hire a contractor to shell it out. We'll pay for the building,

A CONVERSATION WITH AFFILIATE LEADERS   189

and then we'll basically have tenant improvements on every unit. Then, you're running a commercial operation to build houses.

I think if Habitat handles all of that, we're willing to put volunteers on various aspects of it. But as soon as we're handing off liability, insurance, and warranty by signing shell contracts, it becomes a complication that isn't always worth the time. The time it would take to finish with volunteers really diminishes the impact we're going to have in the community. For example, we had a 45-unit building that was going to take us three years to finish out after the contractor shelled it. That's three years to deliver 45 units in an $8 million building we had already paid for, which the general contractor could have finished in three months.

Karen Haycox

We tried every iteration of engaging volunteers in New York City—we built our brand on that. The short version of the story is that we are the Habitat you think you know, as well as this other entity that does multi-family, multistory projects without any volunteer engagement. It remains a challenge organizationally.

We look at what philanthropy the activity would generate during the build phase. We've had to adapt who we are as an organization around how we fundraise. We've had to become much more of a conventional fundraising machine around foundation grants and in asking funders to invest in our capacity. It's a real point of tension because, despite our efforts, we made our bones on the volunteer engagement piece. It's still something that we bring with us, and I love that we do. While [volunteer work] changes hearts and minds, it has really impacted how we fundraise.

Tya Winn

All this manifested across Oxford Green in a scary way. We were tied to funding deadlines by the Housing Authority, and we also had to get a construction draw schedule. We owed the bank money on certain days, and if we hadn't sold a certain number of houses by that date, we were in trouble financially. So, we started subcontracting work out at Oxford

Green. We worked with volunteers on offsite build days, but after that, putting volunteers in the house became a chore for the construction team. It was slowing us down.

Marty Kooistra

I think it's hard. When I came here, the job sites were campsites—they had grills and picnic tables. It was a place for the regular volunteers to take ownership. But, when you looked at the time [from groundbreaking] to market in the fully loaded costs and the burn rate per month—which nobody had calculated until I got here—the units were being subsidized so heavily just to accommodate the culture.

Finding the right ways to utilize volunteers is key. I've always seen the job site experience as the port of entry to get people to understand that they need to be advocates for the kinds of systems change that's going to have results for more than just a few families. It's like we used to say, "Every six minutes we're starting a new Habitat home somewhere around the world. Even at that, we're only 96,000 houses a day short."

Billy Whipple

To go all the way back to that first question—we can do extra energy efficiency things, we can air seal with our volunteers, but it takes a while to get new building officials or new building inspectors on our side. We're Habitat, we're building with volunteers, and the inspectors don't know what they're going to walk into. I try to have a conversation with them and let them know that my labor is free. "If you need more nails or something, let me know." "If you want an extra two by four there, we got some scrap." "I have 30 framers coming tomorrow." After a couple of rounds of that they see that I have zero incentive to cut a corner—I have less of an incentive to cut a corner than your market-rate builder because I need to have people framing tomorrow.

I have 3,000 people walking through the job site every year. They are walking away saying, "Well, this is how Habitat does it." So, we have a huge incentive when we use the volunteers to do it right. It changes your incentive structure a little bit. Siding a gable 35 feet above the ground [with unskilled volunteers] does not make sense, but using volunteers to air seal and using them [on tasks that are] off the critical path does make sense.

It seems that, related to this shift in scale of development, there's been pressure on affiliates to grapple with the idea that they are, in fact, sophisticated affordable housing developers. We know Philadelphia Habitat had to evolve in order to work at the scale the problem demanded. How has the complexity around large-scale development influenced who you need to have on your staff and how you organize your affiliate?

Tya Winn

I saw the shift because Habitat Philadelphia was always considered a big affiliate. For my role, there had always been a preference for someone that was either trained as an architect or as an engineer. When I started at the affiliate, I felt like I walked into a very strong nonprofit. The development team was highly credentialed, the majority of our staff and the development team were good project managers, the associate director and director had MBAs—there was a lot of capacity.

Karen Haycox

I wish I had an easy answer for all of that. Because there are so many complexities to the funding programs that come out of New York City—for which I am highly grateful—we have had to become deeply knowledgeable about how those programs work. We meet with Housing Preservation and Development in New York City multiple times a day. It's become a project management challenge. There's a significant level of sophistication required in terms of the support staff before we even get to the build site.

Due to the underwriting capacity; the strength and understanding of the nuances of the financing models; [and] the long timeline of these multifamily, multistory developments, we try for a two- to three-year window. It really changes the face of the staff because they become program experts, project managers, and financiers in many ways before we even get to a building.

Phyllis Snodgrass

As Karen said, it is a lot more complicated. You don't even start a deal until you figure out the financing. Our finance and construction teams look at the financing for a long time to see if it pencils before we build. Once you get ready to build, you have already done most of the hard work.

We have seen examples of architects being engaged to help resolve difficult sites, negotiate contextual design considerations (historic districts), and provide expertise in energy-efficient design strategies and building typologies (multifamily). Each of you have partnered with very talented design firms to produce the projects we've profiled here. What characteristics do you look for when seeking architects as project partners?

Phyllis Snodgrass

When we looked at Mueller Row, Billy was looking for the architecture firm that would be the easiest to work with. I was looking for the one with the sexiest name that would get us the most recognition, possibly win awards, and have many follow-ups. We have gotten lots of recognition for the project, and Billy will admit—as pained as he was—he learned some things in the process. I know they learned a ton from him and are big fans despite challenges during the process. We had to break out of the mold of what people think Habitat is in Austin.

We've known we could do more. We have projects on the books that are going to look different, but we didn't have anything on the ground yet that represented what we knew we were capable of doing. We're starting to build a portfolio of unique projects, and we're seeing the results now. People are coming to us saying, "I have a little piece of property. Can you put one of your Mueller townhome projects on this strip of land?"

Clients keep going back to that, but we have some other things on the horizon—some different projects with builders and developers and a 126-unit subdivision. As those things roll out, the portfolio of projects they've seen us do will look different.

I think that's really key for Habitat affiliates—changing what they're able to deliver. They need to build that portfolio so that other people know they're capable of doing all these projects. Over 37 years, we've built 507 single-family homes, so that is how everyone knows us. Right now, we are getting stories out on anything we do outside of the single-family house, and we just keep hammering home the message that what we're doing in the future will look different.

Marty Kooistra

We were fortunate to have the right people at Miller Hull that were passionate about [the House of the Immediate Future]. The hardest part is setting the groundwork and understanding the constraints and parameters of the project. We held a 40-person charette with the architects, consultants, the city staff—everybody who was to be involved in that project—before the design was started.

We talked through the fundamental elements and got people in the right headspace philosophically, which was key. It's really important to make sure people understand the fundamentals early on. We want to have an aesthetically pleasing building, we want quality aesthetic detail, we certainly need functional detail, and we want to show that these houses are not second-class homes.

I think it is important to find an architect who wants to take on the challenge of all these constraints, see what they can do within the confines of a smaller structure and a tighter budget, and see how to really use their creative juices.

What are the pros and cons of working with architects that are known for a distinctive portfolio of projects?

Tya Winn

I was really clear when I started that if we were not trying to win design awards, I was not going to last very long. We need to be improving housing because that's why I got into the affordable housing game. I would actually say the biggest pushback was from our family services team. They did not want something that looked better than what we had sold the year before.

When I started, I'd come from the housing authority, and I'd worked in affordable housing in Philadelphia for 10 years at that point. Trying to get support from the surrounding community and the politicians was challenging because council members didn't want Habitat houses in their neighborhoods that would result in complaints from constituents.

ISA [the architecture firm that designed Oxford Green] is a pretty trendy firm, but they are doing a lot of builder-grade work and testing the ideas of what housing could be. We did have some battles because there were some things that they stood firmly about. In many instances, they were correct—it was a better design.

The architect acquired the donations for the facade materials, but we almost said no. We knew it was going to be complicated to install and maintain, and our guys were going to hate it. But we compromised. In the end, the houses look really good. Everybody is really proud of what we did.

We think most architects will tell you that they do their best work when they have a client that can push back against them in an informed and intelligent way. We heard from Michael Hsu's office that Billy's engagement with them was a perfect example of that dialogue. You need someone to say, "I understand what you're trying to do here, but here's another way to get there that's going to work better for us." Could you elaborate on this idea?

Billy Whipple

I think conflict is good. Going back to what Phyllis said, she is right. The collaboration—and conflict—with Michael Hsu's office helped us and pushed us. I think that conversation is centered on knowing what you are trying to do. We were in design on Mueller Row for 18 months. The question was always, "What are we trying to do?"

There's a detail in those white porches where the wall panels are perforated soffits turned vertically with a reveal. Nobody had ever done it, and we would have had a huge liability from a water drainage standpoint. I went to my Hardy representative and admitted that we are not able to do it because we didn't have the tools. They gave us $9,000 worth of saws and vacuums and a $900 rebate on every house, so we had to figure it out. It's really about talking to the designers and trying to figure out the direction they're going and what they want and, as a builder or developer, figuring out how you can get that into your system.

It went the other way, too. There's a window where the header is above the top plate line. As a builder and trained house framer, I had a one-hour argument in their office about how idiotic it was. Through my construction experience and their design experience, we were able to negotiate how that truss came in and how we split the wall panel. We were able to achieve it. I lost, Michael Hsu's office won, and it's beautiful.

Karen Haycox

This returns to your question earlier about the staffing: how does [working with architects] change who we are as a staff? Certainly at points in my career and my project experience, pushing back against a trained architect is not where we come in. That's not what Habitat brings to the table. And as the developer, we have become very good at saying, "Tell me more. Let me understand where we're going. Are we on the same page?" We're getting better at that, but it's a little bit of hard-won experience. You learn later that you should have asked the hard questions.

Our ambition is to reset the expectations of what collaborations between design professionals and Habitat affiliates are capable of producing. In closing, we would like you to draw us back out to broader issues that we haven't directly discussed and give us your perspectives on those themes.

Tya Winn

I think the key is to find a team that supports your cause. We lucked out with ISA. As I had a relationship with them as an architect, I was able to tell them, "I'm not the sole decision maker. You have to get through me, my construction guy, through the development team, and everyone else who has a say, because that's how we work." Once ISA was selected, I really impressed upon them that their team needed to come to a build day. We gave the team a dedicated build day to work with the construction team, so that when we were in design meetings, we had a baseline relationship with each other.

We also made the architects do a charette with the homeowners and homeowner service to understand our systems. We walked ISA through a really intense training at the beginning of the project to show them how we price the house and how if you go above the budget the homeowners can't afford it. By making that really clear up front, it was easier to find partners that care. It's important to get a team that's going to fight for the cause as much as we do.

Phyllis Snodgrass

I think our brand has so much value. We have strongly felt that leveraging the brand and being able to push the envelope and partner with other builders and developers is a big thing we do. They're building the product, and we're just selling it to families who qualify—and we're being a resource to the real estate development community. I think that's been our biggest transition over the last few years—we're getting called to the affordable housing table because of our partnerships and relationships.

The only way that happens is to be above the fold, to get the stories, and to constantly beat it home. We have a 35-year reputation that we are overcoming, and it takes a lot of repetition. Partnering with someone like Michael Hsu makes people think differently about letting us do a project in other parts of town that traditionally wouldn't have been as excited about seeing us. That's critical.

ACKNOWLEDGMENTS

Editor
Designed for Habitat: New Directions for Habitat for Humanity benefitted tremendously from the talents of our editor, Kate Mazade. Her patient, meticulous attention to detail and talents as a writer and editor are reflected on every page.

College of Architecture, Design and Construction Assistance
The authors would like to acknowledge the College of Architecture, Design and Construction SEED Grant Program. The support received through this program helped to make this book possible.

Student Assistants
The authors would like to acknowledge the student research assistants whose efforts helped make this book possible: Molly Campbell, Tate Lauderdale, Britany Noe, and Paige Pennington.

Project Teams
Each case study profiled in *Designed for Habitat: New Directions for Habitat for Humanity* was developed with the assistance of the key project partners. These key participants are identified at the beginning of each chapter. We would like to acknowledge the generous gift of the time they devoted to completing the interviews with the authors and their efforts to assemble the project documentation, illustrations, and photographs. Their enthusiasm for the projects and for helping us share their stories was wonderful. In addition, we'd like to acknowledge the contributions of the project teams that made these projects possible:

Chapter 1
The IVRV House
Project Design Faculty Lead
Darin Johnstone

Student Design Lead
Howard Chen

Winning Student Design Team
Deysi Blanco, Howard Chen, Sarah Mark

Student Design/Development/Construction Team
Louie Bofill, Leonora Bustamante, Howard Chen, Yufan Chen, Hussam Al Dabiani, Jennifer Diep, Eliad Dorfman, Elliot Freeman, Adam Fujioka, Meldia Hacobian, Sungmi Hyun, Thomas Leglu, Sylvia Liu, Ayla Malka, Sarah Mark, Pixy Peng, Noni Pittenger, Jiamin Shou, Cathy Qu, Breeze Xue

Student Seminar Construction Team
Sara Abalkhail, Renso Caicedo, Robert Davidsun, Coleman Griffin, Zhaoji Luo, Xueyang Lyu, Trenton Allan Mays, Saba Nasehi, Nairi Nancy Nayirian, Carol Ann Paden, Uriel Quevedo

Structural Engineer
Nous Engineering; Matthew Melnyk, Principal; Stephanie Miyata

MEP Engineer
ctl-e

Chapter 2
House of the Immediate Future
Design Team
Miller Hull, Architect; Ron Rochon, Partner; Mike Jobes, Design Principal; Chi Krneta, Project Architect; John MacKay, Project Architect; Jim Hanford, Energy

Structural Engineer
Magnusson Klemencic Associates

Landscape Architect
SvR Design

Energy Consultants
Evergreen Certified, Tadashi Shiga, Owner
Z-Home

Mechanical Engineers
Northwest Mechanical
Buzz

Envelope Consultant
RDH Group

Construction Partners
Method Homes, Northwest Mechanical, Sellen Construction, logistics and framing precutting

Developer—Rainier Vista
Dwell Development, Anthony Maschmedt, Principal

In-Kind Contributors
Chi Krneta—photography; Seattle Housing Authority; Weyerhaeuser; Earth Systems NW; Plumbers Without Borders; Gene Johnson Plumbing; Cassie Hibbert—feature light fixture; Silicon Energy; Medallion Industries; Atrium Windows; Daikin Altherma; Atrium Windows; Second Use

Chapter 3
Stevens Street Homes
Buster's House Prototype Design Team
Olivia Backer, Carley Chastain, Ben Malaier, Janine Mwenja

House 66 Student Team
Spring 2018 studio: Lauren Ballard, Meghan Bernhardt, Fox Carlson, Emma Clark, Katherine Ferguson, Jed Grant, Haley Hendrick, Jeff

Jeong, Mary Ma, Kate Mazade, Ashley Mims, Walker Reeves, Rowland Sauls, Jordan Staples, Matthew Wigard
Summer 2018 seminar: Heath Barton, Emma Clark, Noah Dobosh, Melissa Ensley, John Going, Mason Handey, Dee Katoch, Mack Mahoney, Ashley Wiley, Joshua Williams, Valencia Wilson

House 68 Student Team
Spring Studio: Claire Bruce, Justin David, Ozzy Delatorre, Adam Fehr, Jonathan Grace, Emily Hiester, Dongting Huan, Reed Klimoski, Mingtao Liu, Emma Porter
Summer seminar: Erik Aguilar, Carol Allison, Craig Barker, Elizabeth Bowman, Caty Bowman, Zack Burrogh, McClean Gonzalez, Davis Johnson, Emme Mora, Kamron Sullivan, Nieman Ugbesia

Faculty Team
David Hinson, Mike Hosey, Mackenzie Stagg, Elizabeth Garcia

Consultants
David Bitter, CPC; Bruce Kitchell, Phius+ rater; Alexander Bell, energy modeler. The team also received generous assistance from Mark Grantham, Executive Director of the Auburn Opelika Habitat for Humanity affiliate; Jacqueline Dixon, Contractor of Record; Rob Howard of Mitsubishi Electric Heating & Cooling; Alex Cary and Warner Chang from the Institute for Business and Home Safety; Eric Oas of Oasis Heating and Air

Chapter 4
Empowerhouse
Habitat Project Team
Susanne Slater, Executive Director; Andrew Modley, Senior Construction Supervisor; Theresa Hamm-Modley, Project Manager; Dan Hines, Construction Supervisor

Design Team
Laura Briggs, Senior Critic (Parsons, The New School; David Lewis, Professor of Architecture and Dean of The School of Constructed Environments (Parsons, The New School); Joel Towers, Professor of Architecture and Sustainable Design (Parsons, The New School); Jonathan Knowles, Professor (Stevens Institute of Technology)

Chapter 5
Seymour Street
Habitat Project Team
Alex Carver, Harold Strossner, Bob House, Mickey Heinecken, Rob Liotard, Bob Coffey, T. Tall, Dick Cuyler, Peter DeGraff, Peter Forrest, Ken Remsen, Richard McKerr, Kathy Purcell, Bruce Jensen, Mary Lou Webster, Ron Rucker, Bill Johnson, Larry Rowe, Ray Coish, Dave Furney, Ashleigh Hickey, Margaret Carothers, Orli Schwartz, Renney Perry, Clara Wolcott, Dan Kennelly, Doug Way, Greg Moore, James Morriseau, Janice Sabett, John Breen, Lisa Rader, Neil Chippendale, Charlotte Tate, Steve Ingram

Student Team
Nate Albers, Jack Allnutt, Paige Ballard, Calder Birdsey, Kevin Brito, Dula Dulanto, Kevin Ellicks, John Henry Hanson, Reed Martin, Emma McDonagh, Fiona Mustain, Adam Romano, Orli Schwartz, Mireya Sierra, Arturo Simental, Kristine Su, Andreya Zvonar

Faculty
John McLeod

Chapter 6
Booth Woods
Habitat Project Team
Alex Carver, Harold Strossner, Bob House, Mickey Heinecken, Rob Liotard, Bob Coffey, T. Tall, Dick Cuyler, Peter DeGraff, Peter Forrest, Ken Remsen, Richard McKerr, Kathy Purcell, Bruce Jensen, Mary Lou Webster, Ron Rucker, Bill Johnson, Larry Rowe, Ray Coish, Dave Furney, Ashleigh Hickey, Margaret Carothers, Orli Schwartz, Renney Perry, Clara Wolcott, Dan Kennelly, Doug Way, Greg Moore, James Morriseau, Janice Sabett, John Breen, Lisa Rader, Neil Chippendale, Charlotte Tate, Steve Ingram

Student Team: Booth Woods #12 (2019)
Joccelyn Alvarado, Alanna Duncan-Taylor, Noah Fine, Jack Friedman, Erin Hogan, Ella Houlihan, Benjamin Johnson, Amanda Kirkeby, Justin Morande, Jessica Saunders, Sabrina Templeton, Kelsey VanZandt, Jesse Woodhull, Jinghao Zhang, Adreya Zovnar

Student Team: Booth Woods #14 and #16 (2020)
Justin Alkier, Jack Allnutt, Cheryl Engman, Arthur Furniss, Isabelle Gorrivan, Rachel Jeong, Glenn Kontor, Alex Lee, Kyra McClean, Duy Pham, Maria Ramirez, Max Taxman, Nino Tomas, Phumisit Veskijkul, Diego Villanueva, Galen con Wodtke, Clara Wolcott

Student Team: Booth Woods #18 (2021)
Bobbi Finkelstein, Sol Manuel Garza, Will Lee, Magnolia Moskun, Clark O'Bryan, Mano Onni, Sam Segal, Anabel Sesek, Asha Williams

Faculty
John McLeod

Chapter 7
Grand Avenue Duplexes and Basalt Vista
Design Team—Master Planning Basalt Vista
CCY Architects—Rich Carr, AIA, Principal

Design Team—Grand Avenue Duplexes and Basalt Vista
2757 design co.—Erica Stahl Golden, AIA (Principal), Brian Golden (Principal), Thomas Fagan (Architect), Beatriz Soto (Architect), Megan Voiles (Architect)

Landscape Architect—Basalt Vista
Elise Wolf, Connect One Design

Structural Engineer—Basalt Vista
Chris Lytle, CTL Thompson, Inc.

Soils Engineer
James Kellogg, CTL Thompson, Inc.

Civil Engineer—Basalt Vista
Danny Stewart, Roaring Fork Engineering

Mechanical Engineer
August Hasz, Resource Engineering Group

Habitat Project Team
Scott Gilbert (President—Basalt Vista Phase I), Dana Dalla Betta (Construction Manager—Grand Avenue Duplexes and Basalt Vista Approvals), Gail Schwartz (President—Basalt Vista Phases II and III), Jake Ezratty (Construction Manager—Basalt Vista), Habitat for Humanity of the Roaring Fork Valley

Chapter 8
Habitat Quintana
Design Team
Álvarez-Díaz & Villalōn Architecture & Interior Design: Ricardo Álvarez-Díaz, FAIA; Gilberto Ibarra Pérez, AIA; Monique Lugo López, AIA; Gina M. Tormos Aponte; Joaquin Hernández Reyes; Nirmaliz Rodríguez Pérez; Jocelyn Torres Marte

Civil Engineer
Angel E. González Delgado

Structural Engineering
Zapata-Zapata & Associates, PE, PSC

Mechanical Engineering
RAP Consulting Engineer

Electrical Engineering
Juan R. Requena & Associates

Inspector
Norberto Guzmán

Soil Studies
José R. Despiau Ramirez

Contractor
IG Builders Corp.

Habitat Puerto Rico Project Manager
Arq. Rebeca Vicens

Chapter 9
Lomita Avenue Townhomes
Design Team
[au]workshop architects+urbanists: Randy Shortridge AIA (Design Principal); Jason Kersley AIA (Managing Principal); Brian Betsill, AIA (Project Manager/Architect)

Chapter 10
Mueller Row Townhomes
Design Team
Michael Hsu Office of Architecture: Michael Hsu, FAIA, IIDA; Micah Land; Ken Johnson, LEED AP; David Tucker

Landscape Architect
TBG

Metal Fabrication
Boomtown

Structural Engineering
MJ Structures

Masonry
Acme

Cabinetry
IKEA

Tile
Clay Imports

Chapter 11
Oxford Green
Design Team
ISA: Brian Phillips, Deb Katz, Kara Medow, Alex Gauzza, Matt Mayberry

Structural Engineer
Larsen & Landis

Civil Engineer
Cornerstone Consulting Engineers

Landscape Architect
Roofmeadow

MEP Engineer
Stephen Wayland

Energy Star Consultant
MaGrann Associates

Chapter 12
SEED Affordable Housing
Design Team
Karla Rothstein (Principal), Salvatore Perry (Principal), Adam Dayem,
Sean Dawson, Bridget Rice, Hajeong Lim, Fatma Mhmood—
LATENT Productions

Schematic Design Partner
Actual/Office, Adam Dayem (Principal)

Habitat Project Team
Karen Haycox (Chief Executive Officer), Matt Dunbar (Chief Strategy Officer and Executive Vice President), Orlando Marin (Vice President, Real Estate and Construction), Juliana Bernal Guinand (Director of Real Estate Development), and Elizabeth Tietjen (Director of Marketing and Communications)

REFERENCES

Foreword

1 Deutsche Bank Americas Foundation—Living Cities, "The Benefits of Energy Efficiency in Multifamily Affordable Housing," January 2012. https://assets.ctfassets.net/ntcn17ss1ow9/1CuWj5EhCA9nK2RdRZJpF3/3f43e25051c7366eee7208e596463309/DBLC_Recognizing_the_Benefits_of_Efficiency_Part_B_1.10__1_.pdf

2 Geoff Green and Janet Gilbertson, "Warm Front Better Health: Health Impact Evaluation of the Warm Front Scheme." Sheffield Hallam University, May 2008. https://shura.shu.ac.uk/18167/1/CRESR_WF_final%2BNav%2520%282%29.pdf

Preface

1 David Hinson and Justin Miller, *Designed for Habitat: Collaborations with Habitat for Humanity* (New York: Routledge, 2013).

2 Jerome Bagget, *Habitat for Humanity: Building Private Homes, Building Public Religion* (Philadelphia: Temple University Press, 2001), 165.

3 Hinson and Miller, *Designed for Habitat*, xv–xvi.

4 "Habitat Will Move Administrative Offices to Atlanta," *WALB News 10*, April 25, 2006. www.walb.com/story/4812815/habitat-will-move-administrative-offices-to-atlanta. Accessed September 2022.

5 Edwin Hensley (Director of US Construction, HFHI), Amy Anselm (Specialist for Affordable Housing, HFHI), Molly Berg (Senior Specialist of Building Science, HFHI) in video conference discussion with authors, August 2022. Material for this chapter was developed from interviews conducted by the authors with representatives of HFHI.

6 Habitat for Humanity, "Housing and Climate Change: Habitat for Humanity International's Position," September 2022. www.habitat.org/about/climate-change-position

7 Habitat for Humanity, "Habitat for Humanity International and the Home Depot Foundation Announce National Expansion of 'Partners in Sustainable Building'," *Press Release*, August 4, 2009.

8 Hinson and Miller, *Designed for Habitat*, xvii–xx.

9 David Hinson and Justin Miller, "Project 1800," in *Designed for Habitat: Collaborations with Habitat for Humanity* (New York: Routledge, 2013), 118–131. Hinson and Miller, "Project 1800," pp. 118–131, and "Webster Street," pp. 200–219 in *Designed for Habitat*.

10 Your Building Team, "Hiring an Architect." buildingadvisor.com/your-team/architects. Accessed September 2022. While there is little definitive documentation on the involvement of licensed architects in the single-family home market, many sources suggest architects are involved in 1% to 2% of all single-family homes in the United States.

11 Habitat for Humanity, "Habitat Mortgage Solutions." September 2022. www.habitat.org/our-work/habitat-mortgage-solutions

12 Adrienne Goolsby (Sr. Vice President for United States and Canada, HFHI), in video conference discussion with authors, August 2022.

13 Phyllis Snodgrass and Greg Anderson (Habitat Austin), in video conference discussion with authors, October 2019. For more information about Austin's Affordability Unlocked program, visit www.austintexas.gov/department/affordability-unlocked-development-bonus-program.

14 Sam Davis, *The Architecture of Affordable Housing* (Berkeley and Los Angeles: University of California Press, 1995), 17.

Chapter 1

1 Darin Johnstone (faculty member, SCI-Arc) in video conference discussion with authors, December 2020. Darrell Simien (Senior Vice President for Community Development, Habitat LA) in video conference discussion with authors, October 2020. Robert Dwelle (Director of Housing Development and Design, Habitat LA) in video conference discussion with authors, October 2020. Material for this chapter was developed from interviews conducted by the authors with representatives of the project.

Chapter 2

1 Marty Kooistra (Executive Director, Habitat Seattle) in video conference discussion with authors, December 2020. Mike Jobes (Design Principal, Miller Hull) in video conference discussion with authors, December 2020. Brian Abramson (CEO, Method Homes) in video conference discussion with authors, December 2020. Material for this chapter was developed from interviews conducted by the authors with representatives of the project.

Chapter 3

1 Mark Grantham (Executive Director, Auburn Opelika Habitat for Humanity) in discussion with authors, December 2021. Material for this chapter was developed from an interview conducted by the authors representatives from the project, and drawn from the author's direct experience on the project team.

2 David Hinson and Justin Miller, "Chapter 1, DESIGNhabitat 2," in *Designed for Habitat: Collaborations with Habitat for Humanity* (New York: Rutledge, 2013), 2–23. Hinson and Miller, "Chapter 4, DESIGNhabitat 3," in *Designed for Habitat*, 64–81.

3 Justin Miller and Robert Sproull, "DESIGNhabitat 4: Approaching Net Zero energy Affordable Housing," *Grant Report* (Auburn University, 2015).

4 Rural Studio, "20K Busters Home." September 2022. ruralstudio.org/project/20k-busters-home/

5 FORTIFIED—A program of the Insurance Institute for Business & Home Safety, "Home." September 2022. fortifiedhome.org. The FORTIFIED program is a collection of voluntary construction upgrades that work together to protect homes from severe weather damage. The FORTIFIED program was developed by the Insurance Institute for Business & Home Safety (IBHS).

6 David Hinson, Mackenzie Stagg, Elizabeth Farrell Garcia, Rusty Smith, Bruce Kitchell, "Balancing Act: Seeking Equilibrium Between Cost and Performance in Housing Affordability." Proceedings of the *ACSA 110th Annual Meeting*, 2022, expected publication, spring 2023.

Chapter 4

1 The Passive House Institute US has changed its name to Phius. References to Phius standards have been updated where appropriate. Use of the term "Passive House" and "Passive House Institute" reflects the usage applicable at the time the interviews were

conducted with the project stakeholders. "Phius Standards." September 2022. www.phius.org/standards.

2 Laura Briggs, David Lewis, and Joel Towers (Parsons School of Design) in video conference discussion with authors, November 2021. Andrew Modley and Dan Hines (Habitat for Humanity, Washington, DC) in video conference discussion with authors, January 2022. Material for this chapter was developed from interviews conducted by the authors with representatives of the project.

3 US Department of Energy. "About Solar Decathlon." September 2022. www.solardecathlon.gov/about.html. The Decathlon requires teams to preconstruct their houses, disassemble them, transport them to DC, and reassemble them on the Mall; at the conclusion of the competition, they complete the process in reverse and find a location for the home at their institution.

Chapter 5

1 Steve Ingram (President, Habitat for Humanity Addison County) in video conference discussion with authors, December 2021. Ashley Cadwell (Building Committee Chair, Habitat for Humanity Addison County) in video conference discussion with authors, December 2021. John McLeod (Principal, McLeod Kredell Architects) in video conference discussion with authors, June 2022. Material for this chapter was developed from interviews conducted by the authors with representatives of the project.

2 Financial assistance for the solar panels was secured through a set of connected programs including Vermont Low Income Trust for Electricity (VLITE) and the Vermont Housing & Conservation Board (VHCB).

Chapter 6

1 See Chapter 5 Seymour Street.

2 Steve Ingram (President, Habitat for Humanity Addison County) in video conference discussion with authors, October 2021. Ashley Cadwell (Building Committee Chair, Habitat for Humanity Addison County) in video conference discussion with authors, October 2021. Material for this chapter was developed from interviews conducted by the authors with representatives of the project.

3 Island | Mountain Design Assembly, "Home." September 2022. design-assembly.org. Island | Mountain Design Assembly relocated from Penobscot Bay, Maine, to Middlebury, Vermont, during the height of the COVID-19 pandemic to work on Booth Woods.

Chapter 7

1 Jake Ezratty (Construction Manager, Habitat RFV) in video conference discussion with authors, June 2022. Erica Golden (Principal, 2757) in video conference discussion with authors, June 2022. Brian Golden (Principal, 2757) in video conference discussion with authors, June 2022. Material for this chapter was developed from interviews conducted by the authors with representatives of the project.

2 As the team moved toward construction, one of the parcels was sold to a neighbor and the project scope was reduced to two duplexes.

3 Aspen CORE, "Home." September 2022. aspencore.org.

4 Aspen CORE, "About." September 2022. aspencore.org/about.

5 Holy Cross Energy, "History." September 2022. www.holycross.com/history/

6 Habitat for Humanity, "Partners." September 2022. www.habitat.org/about/partners. Habitat for Humanity International has established partnerships for affiliates that include materials, equipment, fixtures, and appliances—as well as partnerships with correctional facilities that train inmates in construction trades (including panelized wood frame wall assemblies).

7 Structural Insulated Panel Association, "What are SIPs?" September 2022. www.sips.org/what-are-sips. SIPs panels are composed of insulation sandwiched between an interior and exterior layer of oriented strand board. The two layers of wood product in the assembly double the cost of the panels.

Chapter 8

1 Amanda Silva (Executive Director, Habitat Puerto Rico) in video conference discussion with authors, October 2021. Ricardo Álvarez-Díaz (Principal, Álvarez-Díaz & Villalön) in video conference discussion with authors, October 2021. Material for this chapter was developed from interviews conducted by the authors with representatives of the project. Álvarez-Díaz & Villalön | Architecture & Interior Design Team and AD&V are registered trademarks.

2 Mercy Corps, "The Facts: Hurricane Maria's Effect on Puerto Rico." Last modified September 2020. www.mercycorps.org/blog/quick-facts-hurricane-maria-puerto-rico.

3 Álvarez-Díaz interview. AD&V agreed to complete the design for the Quintana project on a pro bono basis and were compensated on an "at cost" basis for their construction phase services. The engineering consultants brought to the project by AD&V also agreed to provide services at a cost-of-services fee.

4 Eric Durr, "New York Army Guard Engineers Build Houses in Puerto Rico." News (blog). National Guard, August 17, 2018. www.nationalguard.mil/News/Article/1605141/new-york-army-guard-engineers-build-houses-in-puerto-rico/.

Chapter 9

1 Sonja Yates (Executive Director, SGV Habitat) in video conference discussion with authors, November 2021 and July 2022. Randy Shortridge (Principal, [au] workshop architects + urbanists) in video conference discussion with authors, October 2021. Material for this chapter was developed from interviews conducted by the authors with representatives of the project.

Chapter 10

1 Phyllis Snodgrass (Executive Director, Austin Habitat) in video conference discussion with authors, October 2021. Michael Hsu (Principal, Michael Hsu Office of Architecture) and Ken Johnson (Principal, Michael Hsu Office of Architecture) in video conference discussion with authors, July 2022. Material for this chapter was developed from interviews conducted by the authors with representatives of the project.

Chapter 11

1 Brian Phillips (Principal, ISA) in video conference discussion with authors, September 2021. Tya Winn (Program Manager, PHA) in video conference discussion with authors, January 2022. KC Roney (Executive Director, Philadelphia Habitat) in video conference discussion with authors, November 2021. Material for this chapter was developed from interviews conducted by the authors with representatives of the project.

2 City of Philadelphia, PA. Philadelphia Housing Authority (PHA). *Sharswood/Blumberg Choice Neighborhoods Transformation Plan*. Philadelphia: PHA, 2015. www.pha.phila.gov/media/163410/2015-blumberg_transformation_-_web23.pdf

Chapter 12

1 The New York City Department of Housing Preservation and Development (HPD), "HPD Announces Development Plans for Over 400 Units of Homeownership and Rental Opportunities on 67 Small Vacant City-Owned Lots in Brooklyn, Manhattan, and the Bronx," press release, July 24, 2017, www.habitat.org/about/partners. The New York City Historic Preservation and Development, New Infill Homeownership Opportunities Program (NIHOP) sought to increase affordable housing options by developing small vacant city-owned lots throughout Brooklyn, Manhattan, and the Bronx.

2 Karla Rothstein (principal, LATENT) in video conference discussion with authors, December 2021. Karen Haycocks (CEO, Habitat NYC) in video conference discussion with authors, December 2021. Material for this chapter was developed from interviews conducted by the authors with representatives of the project.

3 City of New York, "Housing New York Final Report," September 2022. www1.nyc.gov/site/housing/index.page. Housing New York plan was an initiative that focused on increasing affordable housing throughout New York City.

4 State of New York, "Homes and Community Renewal," September 2022. hcr.ny.gov. New York Housing and Community Renewal—now Homes and Community Renewal—provides funding for affordable housing in New York State.

5 The New York City Department of Housing Preservation and Development (HPD), "Habitat for Humanity New York City, LATENT Productions, New York State Homes and Community Renewal, New York City Department of Housing Preservation and Development, Community Preservation Corporation Announce "SEED," a Three Building Affordable Development in Brooklyn," press release, March 27, 2017. communityp.com/seed-development-brooklyn/.

Chapter 13

1 Phyllis Snodgrass, Billy Whipple, Karen Haycox, Marty Kooistra, and Tya Winn in video conference discussion with authors, August 2022. Material for this chapter was developed from a panel interview conducted by the authors with representatives of various Habitat for Humanity affiliates. The interview has been edited for clarity.

2 Habitat for Humanity, "Habitat for Humanity International and the Home Depot Foundation Announce National Expansion of 'Partners in Sustainable Building'," *Press Release*, August 4, 2009.

3 Austin Energy, "Austin Energy Green Building." Last modified June 2022. https://austinenergy.com/ae/energy-efficiency/green-building. Austin Energy Green Building, a precursor to the US Green Gold Council's LEED program, was the first green building rating system in the United States.

REFERENCES   205

GLOSSARY

20K Home Program A multiyear design research program based at the Rural Studio. Starting in 2004, successive teams of Rural Studio students have worked within the framework of the 20K Home Program to explore solutions for small, affordable, single-family homes for families in rural western Alabama. Rural Studio. "20K Archives." http://ruralstudio.org/project_tags/20k/.

ADA The acronym ADA stands for The Americans with Disabilities Act, a United States federal civil rights law that prohibits discrimination against people with disabilities in everyday activities. Provisions of the ADA apply to the design of buildings, including certain types of housing, intended to make these environments accessible to people with disabilities. https://www.ada.gov/topics/intro-to-ada/

accessory dwelling unit (ADU) A second, typically smaller, structure that shares a property with another single-family house. An ADU may be a separate structure or attached to the primary house. Legally, ADUs are part of the same property as the primary structure and may not be bought or sold separately.

affordability As used here, the term refers to a contest new to the Solar Decathlon in 2011. The contest encouraged teams to build affordable houses that were evaluated by a professional estimator to determine the construction cost of each team's house entered in the competition. US Department of Energy. "Affordability Contest." DOE Solar Decathlon: Affordability Contest, 2011. www.solardecathlon.gov/past/2011/contest_affordability.html.

AIA Tri-State Honor Award The award is given for projects that exhibit architectural excellence as determined by a jury of peers. The Tri-State Area includes New York State, New Jersey, and Pennsylvania.

American Institute of Architects (AIA) The AIA is a professional organization for architects, emerging professionals, and allied partners in the United States. https://www.aia.org/about

air tightness Refers to a building envelope's resistance to infiltration and exfiltration (air leakage inward or outward). Air tightness has a significant impact on energy loss, mechanical systems sizing, and overall building performance.

California Modernism Used to describe the modernist movement in architecture as it evolved in California, specifically Los Angeles and the area surrounding it, from the 1930s through the 1960s. Hallmarks of this style are attention to indoor–outdoor living, open plans, rectilinear structures often constructed with steel frames, and extensive use of glass. "California Modernism." Docomomo. www.docomomo-us.org/style/california-modernism.

Choice Neighborhoods A competitive grant program administered by the US Department of Housing and Urban Development (HUD) that provides funding for plans aimed at transforming neighborhoods with distressed public or HUD-assisted housing through a comprehensive approach to neighborhood transformation. The program features a two-stage process: a comprehensive neighborhood revitalization strategy (or Transformation Plan), followed by Implementation Grants to support implementation of the strategy. HUD requires that applicants work with public and private agencies, organizations (including philanthropic organizations), and individuals to gather and leverage resources needed to support the financial sustainability of the plan. Tate, Luke. "Fighting Poverty and Creating Opportunity: The Choice Neighborhoods Initiative." US Department of Housing and Urban Development. www.huduser.gov/portal/pdredge/pdr_edge_frm_asst_sec_101911.html.

Computer-based energy modeling tools Software that is used to predict and simulate energy performance of a building design set within a specific location and climate zone.

design charrette A meeting where the participants develop and refine the design and/or planning direction for a project.

double-stud wall system A framing system consists that of two parallel stud-framed walls separated by a gap of varying width, creating an extra-thick cavity that can be filled with insulation. Because the interior and exterior planes of framing are not connected, this approach helps reduce or eliminate thermal bridging.

Energy Star® certified Homes that are designed and evaluated to ensure that the homes meet strict energy performance standards established by the Environmental Protection Agency (EPA). These standards take into account the specific context of the home.

Enterprise Green Communities A green building program focused on housing developments with affordable homes. The program focuses on community involvement in the design process, design focused on moving closer to zero emissions, interior environmental quality, efficiency in water use, and climate resiliency. "Green Communities." Enterprise Community Partners. www.enterprisecommunity.org/impact-areas/resilience/green-communities.

EPA Energy Star standards To be Energy Star certified, a building must meet strict energy performance standards set by the EPA. Specifically, to be eligible for Energy Star certification, a building must earn an Energy Star score of 75 or higher on the EPA's 1–100 scale, indicating that it performs better than at least 75 percent of similar buildings nationwide. This 1–100 Energy Star score is based on the actual measured energy use of a building and is calculated within the EPA's Energy Star Portfolio Manager tool. The score accounts for differences in operating conditions, regional weather data, and other important considerations. "Energy Star Certification for Buildings." ENERGY STAR. www.energystar.gov/buildings/building_recognition/building_certification.

flex house Used to describe flexibility in the use of the rooms of a house by providing spaces that can easily be converted for alternative uses, often a home office or an additional bedroom.

FORTIFIED program A voluntary construction and reroofing program designed to strengthen homes and commercial buildings against

GLOSSARY   207

specific types of severe weather such as high winds, hail, hurricanes, and even tornados. "Fortified Home." FORTIFIED, March 15, 2022. https://fortifiedhome.org/.

Front Porch Initiative A faculty-led endeavor that extends the impact of the design research developed by the 20K Home program at the Rural Studio by working with housing providers outside of the Rural Studio's service area. The Front Porch Initiative harnesses the student prototype designs and develops them into a "product line" of homes. There, the prototype designs are paired with a library of building assemblies to create climate- and client-appropriate houses. The Front Porch Initiative provides both home designs and technical assistance to housing provider partners who, in turn, build the homes in their local communities. "Front Porch Initiative." Rural Studio, February 1, 2020. http://ruralstudio.org/front-porch/.

HVAC The acronym HVAC stands for "heating, ventilation, and air conditioning," and encompasses the various technologies used to control temperature, humidity, and indoor air quality in buildings.

LEED The acronym LEED stands for "Leadership in Energy and Environmental Design," a green building certification program developed by the United States Green Building Council (USGBC). https://www.usgbc.org/leed

low-bono fee A fee for professional services quoted with no, or little profit included. Most commonly used in the context of work performed for nonprofit organizations where the service provider forgoes its normal profit as in-kind support for the mission of the client organization.

MEP The acronym MEP stands for "mechanical, electrical, and plumbing" and encompasses systems and equipments related to thermal comfort, electrical service, and plumbing in buildings.

micro-neighborhood An organization of small houses that create a small community.

modular construction The production of components of a structure in an offsite factory, followed by onsite assembly.

net-zero energy Buildings that produce renewable energy equal to the amount consumed onsite in a given year.

net-zero readiness Buildings designed and constructed to achieve net-zero energy but that do not have the renewable energy system installed. The buildings are wired and ready for the owner to install a renewable energy system. "Zero Energy Ready Homes." Energy.gov. Office of Energy, Efficiency & Renewable Energy. www.energy.gov/eere/buildings/zero-energy-ready-homes.

New Infill Homeownership Opportunities Program (NIHOP) Program that promotes the construction of new homes affordable to New York City's workforce community. NIHOP seeks to promote mixed-income communities with affordable homeownership opportunities for moderate- and middle-income households. Preference is given to projects with one third of the units affordable to households earning up to 80 to 90 percent of the area median income (AMI). Projects may include additional tiers of affordability for households earning between 90 and 110 percent AMI and between 110 and 130 percent AMI. "New Infill Homeownership Opportunities Program." Directory of NYC Housing Programs. NYU Furman Center. https://furmancenter.org/coredata/directory/entry/hpd-new-infill-homeownership-opportunities-program.

Pareto optimal point The point at which no action improves the situation for one individual without adversely affecting another.

Phius A nonprofit organization that promotes and administers a specific, certified, high-performance passive building standards program for buildings and building products. "About Us." Phius. www.phius.org/about-us.

Phius standards Passive building design and construction is centered around key principles: thermal control, air control, radiation control, and moisture control. "Passive Building Principles." Phius. www.phius.org/passive-building/what-passive-building/passive-building-principles.

photocatalytic coating Coatings, such as titanium dioxide (TiO_2), that can be applied to building materials to reduce or eliminate polluted compounds in the air. When compounds such as chlorofluorocarbons (CFCs) come into contact with these coatings, the resulting photocatalytic reaction helps remove these pollutants from the air.

photovoltaic panels Panels that convert the thermal energy from sunlight into electricity. A panel consists of multiple individual cells connected together. The number of cells connected together determines the potential generating capacity of the panel.

Post occupancy energy use The evaluation of energy use once a house has been occupied. Energy use may be monitored at the meter level or at the circuit level.

product line home prototypes See *Front Porch Initiative*.

R-value The measure of how effectively a two-dimensional material, such as a layer of insulation, resists the conductive flow of heat.

radiant floor system A variety of systems that supply heat directly to the floor, which then warms the interior space via radiant heat transfer. Radiant floor heating is more efficient than many other forms of heating, such as electric baseboard heating or forced-air systems.

rainscreen system An exterior cladding material that sits away from the water-resistant layer of a building's exterior wall, creating an air cavity directly behind the cladding, which is vented at the top and bottom of the wall.

re-plat The process of changing the lot, parcel, and easements to allow for the development of a site.

Request for proposal A formal request for a proposal outlining the scope of services, compensation, and schedule associated with professional services, such as the services of an architect or engineer on a building project.

Rural Studio Rural Studio® is an off-campus design-build program located in Hale County, Alabama, and part of the School of Architecture, Planning and Landscape Architecture of Auburn University. Using context-based service learning courses and studies combined with hands-on construction activities by its students, the Rural Studio has built more than 200 projects in the Black Belt of Alabama. "About." Rural Studio, July 11, 2022. http://ruralstudio.org/about/.

smart core A prefabricated modular unit that contains and distributes utilities to the prefabricated and site-erected structure that encases the modular core.

structurally insulated panels (SIPs) Foam insulation layered between two layers of structural board, such as oriented strand board, plywood, or cementitious panels.

thermal bridging The movement of heat through building materials that are more conductive that the surrounding materials, resulting in a path of least resistance for heat. Thermal bridges, such as the wood studs in a conventional wood-framed wall, can be a major source of heat loss in buildings.

Uniform Land Use Review Process (ULURP) The way that land use changes are made, as established as a revision to the New York City Charter. The process involves consultations of the public at the community and borough levels and final determinations by the city council and mayor.

USGBC The acronym USGBC stands for the "United States Green Building Council." The USGBC is a membership-based non-profit organization that promotes sustainability in building design, construction, and operation. The USGBC created and administers the LEED green building certification system. https://www.usgbc.org/about/mission-vision

volatile organic compound (VOC) Chemicals used and residing in many materials and products used to construct and maintain buildings and homes. These materials off-gas into the air inside the building and impact indoor air and environmental quality.

zero-energy homes A home that generally produces as much renewable energy as it consumes over the course of a year.

Zero Energy Ready Home (Zero Ready) A third-party–verified certification program for buildings that are at least 40% to 50% more energy efficient that a typical home, developed by the US Department of Energy. "Zero Energy Ready Homes." Energy.gov. Office of Energy, Efficiency & Renewable Energy. www.energy.gov/eere/buildings/zero-energy-ready-homes.

zoning setbacks The required distance that must be maintained between the property line and the structure as determined and established in a municipality's zoning ordinance.

CREDITS

Chapter 1
1.1 Brittany Noe
1.2 Brittany Noe
1.3 Joshua White/JWPictures.com
1.4 Joshua White/JWPictures.com
1.5 Joshua White/JWPictures.com
1.6 Joshua White/JWPictures.com
1.7 Joshua White/JWPictures.com
1.8 Joshua White/JWPictures.com

Chapter 2
2.1 Brittany Noe
2.2 Brittany Noe
2.3 The Miller Hull Partnership, LLC
2.4 The Miller Hull Partnership, LLC
2.5 The Miller Hull Partnership, LLC
2.6 The Miller Hull Partnership, LLC
2.7 The Miller Hull Partnership, LLC
2.8 The Miller Hull Partnership, LLC

Chapter 3
3.1 Brittany Noe
3.2 Molly Campbell
3.3 Matthew Hall
3.4 Matthew Hall
3.5 Matthew Hall
3.6 Matthew Hall
3.7 Matthew Hall
3.8 Matthew Hall

Chapter 4
4.1 Brittany Noe
4.2 Brittany Noe
4.3 Martin Seck/The New School
4.4 Martin Seck/The New School
4.5 Martin Seck/The New School
4.6 Martin Seck/The New School
4.7 Martin Seck/The New School
4.8 Martin Seck/The New School

Chapter 5
5.1 Brittany Noe
5.2 Brittany Noe
5.3 © Lindsay Selin
5.4 © Lindsay Selin
5.5 © Lindsay Selin
5.6 © Lindsay Selin
5.7 © Lindsay Selin
5.8 © Lindsay Selin

Chapter 6
6.1 Brittany Noe
6.2 Brittany Noe

6.3 © McLeod Architects
6.4 © McLeod Architects
6.5 © McLeod Architects
6.6 © McLeod Architects
6.7 © McLeod Architects
6.8 © McLeod Architects

Chapter 7
7.1 Brittany Noe
7.2 Brittany Noe
7.3 Brittany Noe
7.4 Brittany Noe
7.5 Brian Golden Photography courtesy of 2757 design co.
7.6 Brian Golden Photography courtesy of 2757 design co.
7.7 Brian Golden Photography courtesy of 2757 design co.
7.8 Brian Golden Photography courtesy of 2757 design co.
7.10 Sarah Kuhn Photography courtesy of *Mountain Parent* magazine
7.11 Aerial photography courtesy of Habitat Roaring Fork Valley
7.13 Sarah Kuhn Photography courtesy of *Mountain Parent* magazine

Chapter 8
8.1 Brittany Noe
8.2 Brittany Noe
8.3 Álvarez-Díaz & Villalön® | Architecture & Interior Design
8.4 Álvarez-Díaz & Villalön® | Architecture & Interior Design
8.5 Álvarez-Díaz & Villalön® | Architecture & Interior Design
8.6 Ana Lluch
8.7 Ana Lluch
8.8 Ana Lluch

Chapter 9
9.1 Brittany Noe, Molly Campbell
9.2 Brittany Noe, Molly Campbell
9.3 [au]workshop architects+urbanists
9.4 [au]workshop architects+urbanists
9.5 [au]workshop architects+urbanists
9.6 [au]workshop architects+urbanists
9.7 [au]workshop architects+urbanists

Chapter 10
10.1 Brittany Noe
10.2 Brittany Noe
10.3 Chase Daniel
10.4 Chase Daniel
10.5a Chase Daniel
10.5b Chase Daniel
10.5c Chase Daniel
10.6 Chase Daniel
10.7 Chase Daniel
10.8 Chase Daniel

Chapter 11
11.1 Brittany Noe
11.2 Brittany Noe, Molly Campbell
11.3 Plural VR
11.4 Sam Oberter
11.5 ISA

11.6 Sam Oberter
11.7 Sam Oberter
11.8 Sam Oberter

Chapter 12
12.1 Brittany Noe
12.2 Brittany Noe

12.3 LATENT Productions
12.4 Ho Kyung Lee/LATENT Productions
12.5 Ho Kyung Lee/LATENT Productions
12.6 Ho Kyung Lee/LATENT Productions
12.8 Ho Kyung Lee/LATENT Productions
12.9 Ho Kyung Lee/LATENT Productions
12.10 LATENT Productions

INDEX

20K Home Program 35, 207–208
2757 design co. 82–83

Abramson, Brian 20, 23, 25
Accessory Dwelling Unit (ADU) xx, 5, 188, 207
actual/office 165
ADA 74–75, 207
affordability: conversation with affiliate leaders 186; Empower
     House 49, 51; Glossary 207–208; Mueller Row Townhomes
     134; preface: new directions for habitat for humanity xvii,
     xxiii–xxiv; SEED Affordable Housing 165, 167–168; Stevens
     Street Homes 35
AIA Tri-State Honor Award 153
air tightness 37, 207
Álvarez-Díaz & Villalōn Architecture & Interior Design 102
Álvarez-Díaz, Ricardo 102–103
American Institute of Architects (AIA) 207
Anderson, Greg 132
Auburn University xii, xv, 34, 38, 209
Austin Habitat for Humanity 132
[au]workshop architects+urbanists 116–117

Basalt Vista: Grand Avenue Duplexes and Basalt Vista 82–98;
     preface xviii–xix
Bernal Guinand, Juliana 164, 169
Bitter, David 36
Booth Woods 64, 72–78
Briggs, Laura 48, 50–51

Cadwell, Ashley 60–64, 72–76
California Modernism 116, 207
Carver, Alex 61, 63–64
Catellus Development Corporation (Catellus) 133
Chen, Howard 2, 5–6
Choice Neighborhoods 148–150, 207
City of Glendale Housing Authority 117
Community Preservation Corporation (CPC) 169
computer-based energy modeling tools 36, 207

Dale Corporation 152–153
Dayem, Adam 165
Design Charrette 84, 207
Designed for Habitat: Collaborations with Habitat for Humanity xv
double-stud wall system 24, 207
Dunbar, Matt 164, 168
Dwelle, Ricardo 2–4, 6

Empowerhouse xviii, 48–59
Energy Star®-certified 35, 207
Enterprise Green Communities 165, 167, 207
EPA Energy Star 167
EPA Energy Star Standards 165, 207
Ezratty, Jake 83, 86–89

Flex House 74, 207
FORTIFIED program 37
Front Porch Initiative 35, 208

Gilbert, Scott 84
Goldman Sachs Urban Investment Group 169
Grand Avenue Duplexes 82–85, 89–92, 95–97
Grantham, Mark 34–35, 37

Habitat for Humanity affiliates: Addison County (Vermont) 60–61,
     63–64, 72–76; Auburn Opelika (Alabama) 34–35; Greater
     Los Angeles (California) 3–7; New York City and Westchester
     County (New York) xxii, 164–170; Philadelphia (Pennsylvania)
     148, 150–154, 192; Puerto Rico 102–105; Roaring Fork Valley
     (Colorado) 82–90; San Gabriel Valley (California) 116–119;
     Seattle-King County (Washington) 20–21, 23–25, 185;
     Washington D.C. 49–52
Haycox, Karen: conversation with affiliate leaders 185–197; preface
     xxii; SEED Affordable Housing 164, 167, 170
Hines, Dan 48, 51
Hinson, David 34–39
Holy Cross Energy (HCE) 86
Hosey, Mike 34, 37, 39
House 66 34–43
House 68 34–41, 44–47
House of the Immediate Future 20–28, 194
Hsu, Michael 132–136, 198
HVAC 36, 118, 187, 208

Ingram, Steve 60, 62, 64, 72–76
InVerse-ReVerse house (IVRV) 2–19
ISA 148, 151–152, 154, 159, 197

Jobes, Mike 20–21, 23–24, 26
Johnson, Ken 132, 134–136
Johnstone, Darin 2–7

Kitchell, Bruce 36–37
Kooistra Marty: conversation with affiliate leaders 185–194; House of
     the Immediate Future 20–21, 26

LATENT Productions 164–170
LEED 187, 208–209
Lewis, David 48, 52
Lomita Avenue Townhomes xix, 116–131
low-bono fee 104, 208

Marin, Orlando 164, 168–169
Masterson, Jack 118–119
McLeod, John 60–65, 72–75
McLeod Kredell Architects 60–61, 64, 72–73, 75
MEP 208
Method Homes 20, 22–26
Michael Hsu Office of Architecture 132–133, 195–196
Micro-Neighborhood 73, 75, 208
Middlebury College 60–61, 64, 72–73
Milano School of International Affairs 48–49

INDEX 213

Miller Hull 20–22, 26, 194
The Miller Hull Partnership 20
Modley, Andrew 48, 51–52
modular construction 21–22, 25, 208
Mueller Row Townhomes 132–147

National Renewable Energy Laboratory (NREL) 86
net-zero energy 60, 64, 86–87, 89, 208
net-zero readiness 208
New Infill Homeownership Opportunities Program (NIHOP) 165, 169, 208
The New School 48–49, 52
New York City Department of Housing Preservation & Development (NYC HPD) 164–165, 167

Oxford Green xix–xx, 148–163, 190, 195

Pareto optimal point xiii, 208
Parsons 48–51
Passive House Institute U.S. (Phius) 52, 187, 208
Passive House standards xviii, 36–37, 48, 50–52, 208
Perry, Salvatore 164, 166, 170
Philadelphia Housing Authority's (PHA) Blumberg Apartments 149
Phillips, Brian 148, 151–152, 154
photocatalytic coating 5, 208
photovoltaic panel 4, 104, 208
post occupancy energy use 26, 34, 208
product line home prototypes 35, 208

radiant floor system 24, 208
rainscreen system 23, 208
Reckford, Jonathan x–xiii
re-plat 166, 208
Request for proposal 150, 165, 209
Rochon, Ron 21
Roney, K.C. 148, 150–151, 154
Rothstein, Karla 165–167
Rural Studio 35–36, 207–209
R-value(s) 25, 208

Schwartz, Gail 87
SEED Affordable Housing 164
Sellen Construction 24
Seymour Street 60–71, 73–74
Sharswood 148–150, 152, 154
Shortridge, Randy 116–119
Silva, Amanda 102–106
Simien, Darrell 2–7
smart core 22, 209
Snodgrass, Phyllis: conversation with affiliate leaders 185–198; Mueller Row Townhomes 132, 134–136
Southern California Institute for Architecture (SCI-Arc) 2–7
Stagg, Mackenzie 37–38
Stahl Golden, Erica 82, 84–88
Stevens Institute of Technology 48–49
Stevens Street Homes xii, xviii, 34–47
Steven Winter Associates 167, 169
structurally insulated panels (SIPs) 87–88, 209

thermal bridging 22, 207, 209
Tietjen, Elizabeth 164
Towers, Joel 48, 50

Uniform Land Use Review Process (ULURP) 166–167, 209
US Department of Housing 149, 207
USGBC 187, 208–209

volatile organic compound (VOC) 169, 209

Whipple, Billy: conversation with affiliate leaders 185–196; Mueller Row Townhomes 134
Winn, Tya: conversation with affiliate leaders 185–197; Oxford Green 148–150, 153

Yates, Sonja 116–119

zero-energy homes 49, 209
Zero Energy Ready Home (Zero Ready) 34, 36–37, 208–209
zoning setbacks 62, 209